PREPARE
TO SERVE

WITH ALL YOUR HEART, MIGHT, MIND, & STRENGTH

Missionary Preparation Series-Vol. 1

Marc Stephen Garrison

Orem, Utah

With All Your Heart, Might, Mind, and Strength:
Missionary Preparation Series
ISBN 1-56236-000-0

Volume I: **Prepare to Serve** (ISBN 1-56236-001-9)
Volume II: **Called to Serve** (ISBN 1-56236-002-7)
Volume III: **Continue to Serve** (ISBN 1-56236-003-5)

Published by Aspen Books
893 South Orem Blvd., Orem, Utah, 84058

Prepare to Serve
Second Edition
Copyright © 1990 by Marc Stephen Garrison
All rights reserved
Printed in the United Sates of America
First Edition, August 1988
Second Edition, September 1990
ISBN 1-56236-001-9

Cover design by Stewart Anstead, Aspen Design

Volume discounts available by calling Aspen Books toll-free
1-800-777-8226

Dedication

This series of books is dedicated to Parley P. Pratt, whose missionary zeal inspired me, and to my parents who recognized the gospel message when two Elders knocked on our door. I love you Mom and Dad. I also dedicate this book to each missionary who at the end of a hard day's proselyting has gone on to knock on one more door, to make one more contact.

You are heroes.

When I began writing these books it was for my own children and Hokan and Johan, two young men whose testimonies blaze in the far reaches of Northern Sweden. After several months, I began to realize that I was really writing for anyone who, like myself, truly has desires to serve "With All Their Heart, Might, Mind and Strength."

Acknowledgments

Special thanks to Richard Oscarsson. You were not only a missionary president, you were a friend who taught by example. I thank both you and your wife from the bottom of my heart for serving so diligently in the Sweden, Stockholm Mission. Both you are your family taught me to love missionary work.

Special thanks also to Steve, Joe, Peggy and Nancy for their help and encouragement in completing this book.

Contents

Introduction		Page 1
Chapter 1	Responsibility and Blessings of Serving On a Mission	Page 7
Chapter 2	Qualifications for Serving	Page 23
Chapter 3	Scriptural Preparation	Page 29
Chapter 4	Spiritual Preparation	Page 43
Chapter 5	Mental Preparation	Page 61
Chapter 6	Social Preparation	Page 67
Chapter 7	Financial Preparation	Page 79
Chapter 8	Practical Preparation	Page 91
Chapter 9	Social Ties in Missionary Preparation	Page 99
Chapter 10	Preparation at the Missionary Training Center	Page 107

Introduction

A number of years ago, President Spencer W. Kimball wrote:

When I ask for more missionaries, I am not asking for more testimony-barren or unworthy missionaries. I am asking that we start earlier and train our missionaries better in every branch and every ward in the world. That is another challenge—that the young people will understand that it is a great privilege to go on a mission and that they must be physically well, mentally well, spiritually well, and that 'the Lord cannot look upon sin with the least degree of allowance.'

I am asking for missionaries who have been carefully indoctrinated and trained through the family and the organizations of the Church, and who come to the mission with a great desire. I am asking for better interviews, more searching interviews, more sympathetic and understanding interviews, but especially that we train prospective missionaries much better, much earlier, much longer, so that each anticipates his mission with great joy.

Yes, we would say, every able worthy man should shoulder the cross.What an army we should have teaching Christ and him crucified! Yes, they should be prepared, usually with saved funds for their missions, and always with a happy heart to serve. (Spencer W. Kimball, Ensign, October 1974, pp. 7-8.)

Now the call to missionary service has been extended beyond those who are 19, male and single. The call has been extended also to worthy young women and married couples without children at home.

Remember, young women, you may also have the opportunity to serve a full-time mission. I am grateful my own eternal companion served a mission in Hawaii before we were married in the Salt Lake

Temple, and I am pleased that I have had three granddaughters serve full-time missions. Some of our finest missionaries are young sisters. (Ezra Taft Benson, *Ensign*, November 1986.)

Let me encourage you faithful married couples without children at home to go on missions. The Lord needs you out in the mission field. Forget your fears. We don't expect you to do everything the young missionaries do. (Elder Robert E. Wells, *Ensign*, November 1985.)

The purpose of this book is to help prospective missionaries gain an understanding of the responsibility and blessings of missionary service, increase their desire to serve, alleviate fear or apprehensions, learn and refine missionary-related skills, and to show how a mission can remain a very real part of your life after you return. I haven't tried to candy coat anything. But instead I have tried to honestly portray missionary work as it is, as it can be, and as it will be if you prepare now. Missionary service can be one of the most exciting and enjoyable experiences of your life if you choose to make it so.

Several weeks ago my father and I boarded a jet and flew to Chicago, then New York and on to Oslo, Norway. Getting off the plane, we were greeted by bitter cold and penetrating, gusty winds. After renting a car, we drove to a small town outside of Oslo to visit a lady I had baptized in Sweden several years earlier. As we arrived at her home, my thoughts leaped back over the years.

As a young missionary, I had been given as my first area a small town in Sweden where there hadn't been missionaries since World War II. Opening the town was tough, but my companion and I decided to dig in and really work. We spent the next few days making contacts in the community and even having an article about us printed in the local newspaper. A group of preachers responded with some really negative articles about us, but the Swedes, being the independent thinkers that they are, instead of turning against us viewed us as heroes.

We felt inspired one cold night to tract in a certain apartment complex. We knocked on a particular door and were greeted by a young mother of two children. As she opened the door, we went into our standard door approach. She said she wasn't interested at all in a family home evening program. As she started to close the door, the words blurted out of my mouth, coming apparently from nowhere, "Would you like to know about the meaning of life? Would you like to know where you lived before this life and where you are going to go afterwards?" She stopped and stared at us. Words could not convey the feelings she had. We knew that the spirit had touched her.

As we taught her that night, the weather, the snow, the cold, our apartment with the outdoor outhouse, were all forgotten as we communed with the spirit. Our tongues were loosened as we taught her the plan of salvation and introduced this fine young woman to Joseph Smith and the Book of Mormon and the plan of salvation.

Several weeks later, as we baptized her in a small swimming pool in the area, we felt the true fruits of missionary work. Now, ten years later, I pulled our rental car in front of this lady's house not knowing what to expect. Her children had grown; what were they doing, who was I to intrude? We knocked on the door and were welcomed warmly. As we talked it seemed like Christmas. She told how she had been through the temple and how she was in the Relief Society presidency of the local ward. Her daughter told about how she was president of her seminary class, and her son talked about how he was getting ready for a mission.

My Dad, not understanding a word, sat quietly on the sidelines, perceiving through the spirit what we were talking about. He shared in empathy with this beautiful family as I told them how, when I was a boy, two missionaries had knocked on our family's door and through love and devotion had taught us the gospel.

As I sat that night after everyone had gone to bed, I couldn't help thinking how simple the gospel is, how glorious is its message, and how utterly important missionary work is. If those two Elders who taught my parents had given up, where would I be now? Where would this family, and other families that my father had taught as a stake missionary and I as a full-time missionary, be?

Prepare to Serve

Several days later my father and I sat in the Stockholm Temple in a marriage sealing room with another that I had taught, a beautiful Swedish girl who was the original reason for our trip. She had recently met a handsome young Swedish man and introduced him to the Gospel. On this day, November 27, this couple were to be sealed for time and eternity as man and wife. As the ceremony was performed, my mind seemed to be filled with a marvelous light. I saw myself not as this girl's missionary, but as her friend.

I went home from that trip grateful to the Lord for having called two missionaries to teach my family and for having good teachers who helped steer me through my youth. I was grateful also for having been so blessed as to have been able to serve a full-time mission, to have been able to feel that spirit, to have been able to apply the success principles I learned on my mission in my business life and to have been able to keep my mission alive after my return.

This three-volume set of books has not been written by someone who knows everything about missionary work, but by someone who loves missionary work with his whole heart. I feel an almost desperate need to share my thoughts about the importance of preparation, better allegiance to your call and a continuation of the spirit of your mission after you return home.

In preparing these ideas I have relied on not only my own experiences, but also the experiences of other returned missionaries, the encouragement of my family, and the light and guidance which the Lord promises those who seek his help through humble prayer.

These three volumes of *With All Your Heart, Might, Mind and Strength—Prepare to Serve, Called to Serve, Continue to Serve*—contain a series of chapters concerning the 21 phases of missionary work that I have defined, each beginning with a true story of missionary work. I thank those who have shared these stories with me. Since many of these stories are quite personal, I am only going to include each missionary's first name and their mission. I could have chosen stories that disregarded the tough side of missionary work, but I've always disliked people who told me things were easy when they turned out to be hard. I hope that all who read these books before their missions will enter the mission field realistically prepared for the great work that they are called on to do, and that they will go knowing that sometimes it will be hard, but that they can still serve a successful mission because of the great help they will receive from the Spirit.

As you read these books, take the time to look up and ponder each scripture that I mention. Make notes in the space provided about how the scripture relates to your own missionary service. I would enjoy having you share your missionary experiences with me, too.

My hope is that each person who reads these books, whether they be a Missionary Couple, Sister, Elder or missionary member will feel the spirit and joy of missionary work and commit themselves to serving as the Lord directs, "with all their heart, might, mind and strength."

>My best,
>Marc Stephen Garrison
>893 South Orem Blvd.
>Orem, Utah 84058

Note for Parents: Taken individually each of the stories and chapters from these three volumes could be used as the basis for family home evenings. For example, starting with Book I — *Prepare to Serve*, Chapter 1, you might base a family home evening around the concept of "The Responsibilities and Blessings of Serving on a Mission." You could begin the lesson by singing a missionary song such as "Ye Elders of Israel", then have someone read the true story which the chapter begins with. After reading the story you could review and discuss the ideas that are described in that particular Chapter. Depending on the age of your children, individual scriptures and reports could be assigned to be read from that chapter. The remaining twenty Chapters could be used for the next twenty weeks, or mixed in with other activities or lessons depending on your family's needs.

Prepare to Serve

Note for Missionary Preparation Teachers: Chapters can be combined and used for a 12 week missionary preparation course. Each prospective missionary should have read each of the designated Chapters prior to each meeting. Individual reports and assignments could be derived from each of the lessons. Group discussion and role play would be an integral part of using these chapters as learning tools.

Book I — *Prepare to Serve*

Week 1	Chapters 1 and 2
Week 2	Chapters 3 and 4
Week 3	Chapters 5 and 6
Week 4	Chapters 7 and 8
Week 5	Chapters 9 and 10

Book II — *Called to Serve*

Week 6	Chapters 1 and 2
Week 7	Chapter 3
Week 8	Chapter 4
Week 9	Chapters 5 and 6
Week 10	Chapters 7

Book III — *Continue to Serve*

Week 11	Chapters 1, 2 and 3
Week 12	Chapter 4, Review and Testimony meeting

Chapter 1

Responsibility and Blessings of Serving on a Mission

Hold yourself responsible for a
higher standard than anybody else
expects of you. Never excuse yourself.

        Henry Ward Beecher

Scriptures:
D & C 84:80, D & C 31:3, 1 Thessalonians Chapter 2

Sister Whitney
Austrian Mission

   My story is a little different than most. I didn't sing songs about going on a mission when I was in Primary and I didn't have a Bishop call me into his office to ask me to serve a mission. In fact, I was never in Primary, and when I decided to go on a mission, I had to go to some effort to find a Bishop. I was baptized by two missionaries who originally approached me in a grocery store. It was cantaloupes more than the Gospel that brought us together that first time. I was walking through the produce section when I noticed these two guys dressed in suits having a disagreement over two cantaloupes. I guess they figured that since I was a girl, I was qualified enough to settle the dispute. I had no sooner gotten a cantaloupe in each hand than one of them asked,

"What do you know about the Mormons?" I thought it was another produce question, at first. When they saw me looking blankly at the bins of fruit, the other one said, "The church, the Mormon Church." Before long, these young men had sparked my curiosity in a church that could inspire a nineteen year old guy to spend two years in some unfamiliar place wearing suits and riding bicycles.

After a couple of emotionally and spiritually intense weeks of discussions, I began to understand who I really was, and I accepted the baptismal challenge with tears in my eyes. The nearest branch of the Church was over an hour away from where I lived, so the elders were the only members I was able to get to know at first. Several sweet members showed up at my baptism and I attended church a few times, but I didn't have a lot of close contact with members.

Shortly after my baptism, I decided to return to college. Now that I had the Church, life was beginning to make a lot more sense, and finishing school seemed like the right thing to do. At college, I expected to see even fewer Mormons. To my surprise, however, during the first week I spotted an advertisement for LDS institute classes. The Institute ended up being five students and a teacher meeting in a room on campus, but it was exciting to meet other Mormons my own age. We all became immediate friends, and there was one girl in particular that I grew really close to. I was surprised one day to find out that she had served a mission in South America. I didn't know that girls could go on missions. From that day on, I began to think more and more about missions. The idea absolutely terrified me. I was in college and things were really going my way. The last thing I wanted to do was to leave everything and go on a mission, and, yet, I couldn't shake the thought from my head. It kept following me and would catch up with me in the oddest places. I would be studying in the library or attending class, and all of a sudden I would get this roller-coaster feeling in my stomach. All the while, I was trying to fight it off. One night, I was at a McDonald's restaurant with my friend from the institute class, and I suddenly started crying. I recognized the same feeling that I had when I prayed about being baptized. I knew that God wanted me to go on a mission. When I told my friend, she started crying, too. When we realized how ridiculous we must have looked, two crying girls in the middle of McDonald's, we both laughed uncontrollably.

The next step was to find a Bishop and get things started. I still had a few more months before I would be eligible to serve a mission, since I hadn't yet been a member for a year. I used this time to save money and prepare. The first thing the stake president asked me was why I wanted to go. This was a tough question. I felt that I should come up with some really spiritual answer about how I wanted to bless the lives of my fellow men and to save the world, but in reality, I couldn't truthfully say that I wanted to go on a mission. I explained to the stake president that I wasn't sure why I was going, but I had felt the Holy Ghost, and I knew the Lord wanted me to serve a mission. The stake president then replied that was probably the best possible answer to his question. He went on to relate the story of Adam, when he was offering sacrifices after being kicked out of the Garden. An angel came down and asked Adam why he was offering sacrifices. Adam said, "I know not, save the Lord commanded me." The stake president said that obedience was one of the greatest gifts we could give to our Father in Heaven. I knew then that, more than anything else, I wanted to give this gift to my Father.

As an added blessing, my two missionaries and I were able to correspond throughout my mission. Since they were quite "green" when they taught and baptized me, we were all three serving in the mission field at the same time. We were able to share mission experiences, and, they – especially the one who felt that his mission was not too successful – were able to feel the influence of their missions extended through mine.

In my first area, we taught a young man who was confused about life and not very happy. I watched as the Gospel transformed his life. After his baptism he became a different person, excited about life and the new knowledge he had been given. It wasn't long before he, too, decided to go on a mission. When he left for his mission, I was still serving mine, and we were able write to each other. I felt then the joy my own two missionaries must have felt in having one of their converts enter the mission field. It thrilled me to read of his experiences and about the families he was able to teach. I thought back to the sad young man on whose doorstep I had stood just a short year ago. I thought back even further to that fateful day in the grocery store, when the Gospel entered my life in the unassuming guise of two young missionaries arguing over cantaloupes.

I thank my Heavenly Father for the miracle of missionary work. I have seen the Gospel change lives as the torch of missionary responsibility has been passed from one hand to the next. The blessings of a mission extend into the eternities, for both the convert and the missionary.

• • •

Some 2,700 years ago, the prophet Amos envisioned "a famine in the land, not a famine of bread, nor a thirst of water, but of hearing the words of the Lord." This became a reality in the grimmest sense during that period we call the great apostasy, when the world rejected the Gospel truths Christ had brought. After many long centuries of darkness, the Gospel has been restored, yet most of the world remains in its starving condition. The Savior's final charge to His disciples in an earlier yet similar situation now falls to us:

> *Go ye therefore, and teach all nations, baptizing them in the name of the Father, and of the Son, and of the Holy Ghost: teaching them to observe all things whatsoever I have commanded you: and lo, I am with you always, even unto the end of the world.*
> (Matthew 28:19-20.)

"But, why me?" you might ask. Your mission can actually be thought of as an inheritance tax, of sorts. If you were given a couple of million dollars as an inheritance, you would be required to give part of it back in taxes. Well, your patriarchal blessing probably has (or will have, if you haven't gotten it yet) announced your lineage in the house of Israel and promises you the inheritance blessings that go with that heritage. All this goes back to Abraham, back to the times of the Old Testament. Abraham was so righteous that God made some very important promises to him. We call those promises the Abrahamic covenant. Abraham was promised salvation and eternal life and that all of his mortal posterity would have the opportunity to achieve these same blessings. You are that posterity. Abraham was also told that through his seed all nations of the earth would be blessed. The missionary work is the tax on all those blessings. The Lord said to Abraham, ". . . thou shalt be a blessing unto thy seed after thee, that in their hands they shall bear this ministry and Priesthood unto all nations." (Abraham 2:9) As descendants of Abraham in the house of Israel, we are partakers of the covenants God made with him. God will fulfill his part of the covenant, but our part is to carry the gospel message to all the world, thereby blessing all nations.

The gospel writer Luke tells us that where much is given, much is required. We have been given the fullness of the Gospel with all of its wonderful blessings, and it is required of us to share it with the rest of the world. What is wonderful is that the "tax" which is required of us also happens to be one of our greatest blessings. The opportunity to serve a mission and to bring the life-changing influence of the gospel to others is sacred and important. Indeed, missionary work is the most important work being done on the earth today. And you can be a part of it!

In an address to a large group of seminary and institute students, President Ezra Taft Benson made the following remarks:

Make no mistake about it, you are a marked generation . . . .

There has never been more expected of the faithful in such a short period of time than there is of us.

Never before on the face of this earth have the forces of evil and the forces of good been so well organized . . . .

Prepare to Serve

While our generation will be comparable in wickedness to the days of Noah, when the Lord cleansed the earth by flood, there is a major difference this time: God has saved for the final inning some of His stronger and most valiant children, who will help bear off the kingdom triumphantly . . . .

You are the generation that must be prepared to meet your God. (Ensign, April 1979 p. 73.)

You are the strong and valiant children of God that President Benson referred to. You are the hope of this generation. Your responsibility to serve a mission is based on commitments you made in the pre-earthly world. It's all up to you, now. President Benson, while speaking at a Christmas devotional, said that "Men are tried and tested in this mortal probation to see if they will put first in their lives the kingdom of God." In that same devotional, he said "Nothing is going to startle us more when we pass through the veil to the other side than to realize how well we know our Father and how familiar his face is to us." If we could only remember our pre-mortal life and the way we felt about the gospel when we were there. If we could only remember our great desire to please our Father and the promises we may have made there to others to bring them the gospel on Earth. If only we could see how tall and noble we stood there. Maybe then we wouldn't let worldly cares and selfish desires keep us from doing what we came here to do. Maybe then Satan wouldn't be able to use the veil to his advantage by whispering in our ears that we are less than what we really are. Maybe then he wouldn't be able to persuade us to settle for less than what has already been promised us by a loving Father. That is how Satan cheats our souls.

It's like a popular game show I used to watch as a kid. The host would walk up to some ridiculously-costumed contestant and hand him a hundred-dollar bill. He would then give the contestant the option of keeping the hundred dollars or trading it for some unknown prize hidden behind a curtain. If the guy decided not to risk it and to just settle for the cash, the curtain would be drawn, invariably revealing some fancy sports car that he'd just passed up.

You're now at a point in your life where you have to make a similar decision to that contestant's. You've been asked to devote one to two years of your life to serving a mission. Do you hang on to what you already have — girlfriend/boyfriend, school, car, grandkids — or are you willing to trade it for something you can't see at the moment. Old settle-for-less Satan would have you believe that a girlfriend in the arms is better than a mission in the bush. Missions are a little scary because there's no way of knowing exactly what to expect, but don't let anyone fool you: behind that curtain to the future lies unspeakable opportunities.

"But what is a mission and what will it require of me?"

Missionary work is people work; it requires a missionary to become a people expert. Rather than trying to convert people through the mass media or some other impersonal manner, the Lord has asked that real people — young men and young women and more mature couples — go forward, and in a very personal way, teach the gospel of repentance. It is through the people-to-people efforts of missionaries and members of the Church that the gospel becomes a visible day-to-day way of living for investigators instead of an abstract principle. Through testimonies borne by real voices and living examples demonstrating the fruits of righteous living, nonmembers of the Church are able to grasp the teachings of the Savior, feel the warmth of the Spirit, and gain the courage to live true and rewarding principles. Missionaries of the restored Gospel introduce them to a true worship of the Lord who said, "I am the bread of life: he that cometh to me shall never hunger; and he that believeth on me shall never thirst." (John 6:35.)

The Lord's love for each person on this earth is great. Because of this love, He allowed His Son to suffer for the sins of all men and women that they might not suffer everlasting punishment for their sins if they would but repent. Consider the Lord's words to Oliver Cowdery and David Whitmer in 1829:

Prepare to Serve

Remember the worth of souls is great in the sight of God; For, behold, the Lord your Redeemer suffered death in the flesh; wherefore he suffered the pain of all men, that all men might repent and come unto him. And he hath risen again from the dead, that he might bring all men unto him, on conditions of repentance. And how great is his joy in the soul that repenteth! (D&C 18:10-13.)

For those of us who find it a challenge even to love those who love us (such as our family and friends) it may be difficult to understand this love for others. Often as Latter-day Saints we think of ourselves as an elect and chosen people. But we forget that every person — even the man or woman we don't like or understand — is a literal child of our Father in Heaven. He takes a father's interest in each person's happiness and development. The lives of others may not hold much interest for us, but they are of intense interest to the Lord, who notes the fall of every sparrow and numbers the hairs of each person's head. While this charity may be hard for us to fully grasp, many missionaries have been able to acquire this same deep and abiding love for their brothers and sisters. The Book of Mormon tells us how the sons of Mosiah trembled at even the thought that one person should suffer eternal damnation (Alma 28:3). Because of their love for the Lamanites (their nation's enemies) the sons of Mosiah labored for fourteen years among the Lamanites and suffered many hardships in the hopes that they might bring "some few of their souls" unto repentance and back to their Father in Heaven (Alma 26:26,30).

Because of the Lord's love for men and women, He has promised great blessings to those who diligently strive to bring souls unto him. In the Doctrine and Covenants, Jesus Christ promises great joy in His Father's Kingdom to those who will bring even one soul unto repentance (D&C 18:16). He also promises missionaries that they will be able to continue their friendships with converts into the eternities (D&C 15:5-6). In addition, faithful ambassadors of Christ are promised that a multitude of their sins will be forgiven and forgotten (D&C 62:3).

Because of His love for all mankind and His love for missionaries themselves, the Lord has issued the call for worthy members to serve a mission.

Prepare to Serve

The question is frequently asked: Should every young man fill a mission? And the answer has been given by the Lord. It is 'Yes.' Every young man should fill a mission. He said:

'Send forth the elders of my church unto the nations which are afar off. . . ; unto the islands of the sea; send forth unto foreign lands; call upon all nations, first upon the Gentiles, and then upon the Jews.' (D&C 133:8.)

He did not limit it.

The answer is 'yes.' . . . Every able worthy man should shoulder the cross. What an army we should have teaching Christ and him crucified! (Spencer W. Kimball, *Ensign*, October 1974, p. 8.)

In addition to every young man, the call has also been extended to interested worthy young women and to mature couples without children at home to go on missions. Let me repeat two quotes about the importance of young women and couples serving as missionaries.

Remember, young women, you may also have the opportunity to serve a full-time mission. I am grateful my own eternal companion served a mission in Hawaii before we were married in the Salt Lake Temple, and I am pleased that I have had three granddaughters serve full-time missions. Some of our finest missionaries are young sisters. (Ezra Taft Benson, *Ensign*, November 1986.)

Let me encourage you faithful married couples without children at home to go on missions. The Lord needs you out in the mission field. Forget your fears. We don't expect you to do everything the young missionaries do. (Elder Robert E. Wells, *Ensign*, November 1985.)

Of course this service has a dual purpose. Not only will missionary work bring people to the joy of the gospel, but it will also bring great blessings into the lives of missionaries. Consider carefully the following words of one of the Lord's modern-day servants.

15

Again, ask yourself, "Could they apply to me?"

Missions are for missionaries. It is a marvelous gift of time, a time given when you can experience glimpses of heavenly life here on earth. It is a time of cleansing and refreshing. It is a special time when the Holy Ghost can seal upon you the knowledge of the great plan for your exaltation.

It is one of your best opportunities to become a celestial candidate. (Elder William R. Bradford, *Ensign,* November 1981, p. 51.)

It's hard to imagine ourselves as glimpsing heavenly life here on earth. But I know that missionary work can bring a bit of heaven into each of our lives. Let me illustrate. On one particularly cold night in Sweden, my companion and I were riding our bikes in a severe snow storm out to teach a lesson to a part member family. Because of the heavy rush hour traffic, we were forced to ride in the shoulder area of the road where the snow was piled to great depths. The normal one-hour bicycle ride to this family's home seemed as if it would never end. On the outskirts of their town, we pulled our bikes off into a snow bank then walked out in the woods to pray. The storm had cleared and the stars and moon shown down from the dark sky. As we knelt in prayer, we asked the Lord to inspire us to touch this family's father. We ended our prayer and quietly made our way to the home. Peace settled over us. Our doubts had fled, and we knew that we were led by the Spirit. That night we said and did things and discovered reasons that we had never before considered for this man's reluctance to join the Church. We answered many of his unvoiced concerns, and in a moment of privacy, directly confronted the father. As we left that night, we again pulled our bikes off the road and sought the Lord in prayer. We prayed that our efforts would be accepted by the Lord. That night in the forest, knee-deep in snow, we felt the warmth of the Lord's Spirit. Because of his experiences that night, the father allowed his children to be baptized, and soon he was to join his family in membership in the church.

It is difficult to describe the feeling of being so close to the Lord that you can be an instrument in His hands. That, to me, is one of the best examples of having a personal glimpse of heaven here on earth. I know missionary work is one of the best ways to experience that feeling. It is the most humble form of service that exists. I also have a testimony that through missionary service we can truly become heroes and actually change other lives. I often hear people who say that they want to do something big in the world. I know of nothing bigger than bringing the gospel into someone else's life.

A missionary's main responsibilities are to find people to teach, teach people the gospel, and baptize people who accept the gospel. They also train members in missionary work and may teach inactive families, as invited by local leaders. In order to perform these duties effectively, a missionary must be well prepared. The purpose of this book is to assist you in your own personal preparation to serve a mission.

One who honorably fulfills a calling as a missionary must want to do the work and succeed in it. Are you ready and willing to "seek first the kingdom of God"? To be set apart for a time from the normal pursuits and ambitions and associations of your life? To give your whole heart, mind, strength, and loyalty to the sacred cause? Will you commit yourself for the rest of your life to the high standards of responsibility and devotion expected of one who has been a missionary? If your answers are affirmative, your foundation is firm; if they are not, it is time for you to prepare.

Since preparation is vital to success in almost every endeavor, it is essential that young men and women as well as older couples prepare for their time of service. Often prospective missionaries feel that if they attend their meetings and read their scriptures then they are adequately preparing for their missions. Unfortunately, many fail to realize that missionary service is the most demanding work they will ever do. It is appropriately called missionary work — for the call requires that the missionary labor through two years of fourteen-hour days filled with tremendous emotional, mental, spiritual, and physical challenges. For example, as a missionary you may be asked to face bad weather, endure unhealthy living conditions, learn a foreign language, ride a bike for an hour in the rain, or stand on a corner and preach a message to a hostile crowd. And that may be just the first day! A mission is no vacation. But as great as the challenges of a mission are, a prepared missionary can overcome them — and have fun doing it!

President Spencer W. Kimball has said that there is no greater bondage than service without joy. Missionary service can be a form of bondage if a missionary fails to prepare. Take for example the simple challenge of eating well. Missionaries are notorious for, well, shall we say, monotonous diets. Many returned missionaries speak of eating rice and beans, fast food, or spaghetti three or more times per week. Why? Returned missionaries say they often ate the same meals over and over because it was quick, inexpensive and about all they knew how to make.

But such repetitious and unbalanced diets are so unnecessary!

A prospective missionary who will take the time to prepare for the challenge of eating well can enjoy great variety and nutrition in his meals. A prospective missionary who will take a few hours to compile and learn to make two weeks worth of recipes for quick, inexpensive and nutritious meals will have a much easier time in the mission field. He will eat better, stay healthier, be in greater demand as a companion, and will simply enjoy his mission more.

This type of preparation is so simple, yet it can have a major effect on every aspect of your mission experience. If, as a prospective missionary, you will take a mere hour each week to practice teaching the missionary discussions with a friend, you will be ready to answer those inevitable tough investigator questions and be better qualified to teach with the Spirit. If you will take the time to anticipate types of companionship friction that may arise, you will be better able to smooth things over when it is "your turn" to wash the dishes for the second day in a row.

Beyond being solely a time to teach the gospel a mission can be a genesis for a successful future life in business and the church.

Prepare to Serve

When you arrive at the Missionary Training Center (MTC), you will be given a lot of material. Among the materials will be a little, white booklet that has come to be known as the "white bible." This is the Missionary Handbook. It is an important reference and contains essential information that you will refer to almost daily on your mission. It would be useful for you to obtain and review a copy of the Missionary Handbook before you enter the mission field. Pages 3-5 discuss the importance and responsibilities of your calling. "You represent the Lord and his Church, the only church with the authority to baptize those who will believe and repent . . . . Give dedicated service, and your mission experience will bring you closer to the Lord and strengthen you spiritually for the rest of your life."

For a future family home evening, show the film *Go Ye into All the World* (30 minutes). If the film is not available from your local ward or branch, you might invite a recently returned missionary to attend your family home evening to share some of his experiences and his testimony.

If you were to go on a trip across the country in your car, you would probably spend weeks getting everything ready, packing, checking the tires, lining up hotels, and planning your route of travel. Missionary work is no different. To have a successful experience, you have to prepare. Missionaries who don't prepare waste the greater part of their missions just getting up to speed to become effective servants of the Lord. I have a testimony of the great joy that can come while preparing for a mission. When I was getting ready myself, it was so easy to get caught up the "busy work" of getting shots and going shopping for clothes. But, the quiet moments with my bishop, family, friends and other returned missionaries helped channel my mission preparation into a productive purpose.

By now you are anxious to receive your mission call. There are few moments as exciting as that moment when you go to the mailbox and find that letter from Salt Lake City calling you to serve. But before you can even begin to wait for your call, there are a few items that you need to take care of months before you can even submit your missionary papers.

Your Mission Call

Once you have decided to serve a mission it would advisable right from the start to have a talk with your bishop. He can answer many questions regarding the how's and when's of a mission, as well as get you started on the necessary paperwork. He can help you set some realistic goals that will help in your preparation. He can also give you some perspective.

When you meet with your bishop, frankly discuss any physical, emotional, or financial problems that you feel may restrict you in your missionary service. Your bishop can help you find a way to deal with such challenges before you leave so that your time in the mission field can be happy and productive. Before receiving your call you will be required to take a language proficiency test to assess your ability to learn a foreign language. In addition, you will be required to pass a physical examination with your doctor to ensure that you are physically capable of dealing with the demands of mission life. After you have completed these items you will be interviewed by your bishop and stake president. These men can be a tremendous strength to you during this preparatory time. They can answer questions about missions, determine your worthiness to serve, and discuss any financial or health restrictions that may apply. In subsequent interviews they will also interview you for a temple recommend in order that you may receive your temple endowments. Don't be shy about asking questions during these interviews. This is one of only a few times before your mission when you will have a chance to discuss your coming service one-on-one with wise and experienced leaders.

I know that you can be a successful missionary. I have a feeling that many people avoid missionary service because they feel they don't know everything. The Lord doesn't call people who are always one-hundred percent ready. Part of the blessing of your calling is the growth that you will experience as you prepare. I recently received a church calling to serve in the temple which I felt very inadequate to fulfill. As I received my call and was set apart, I was blessed with the ability to learn and to be able to perform my calling. As those words were pronounced, my heart soared as I felt the loving spirit of our Father in Heaven who blesses each of us with just what we need. I personally know that the Lord will bless you in your efforts to prepare for your missionary service.

For those who feel that other things might be more important than missionary service, let me share with you what our prophet has said.

The Lord wants every young man to serve a full-time mission. Not only should a mission be regarded as a priesthood duty, but every young man should look forward to this sacred privilege — to serve the Lord for two years with all your heart, might, mind and strength. You can do nothing more important. School can wait. Scholarships can be deferred. Occupational goals can be postponed.

Yes, even marriage should wait until after a young man has served an honorable full-time mission for the Lord. Young men, look forward to full-time missionary service. Show your love and commitment to the Lord by responding to His call to serve.
(President Ezra Taft Benson, *Ensign*, May 1986.)

I'd like to share with you one more thought about the blessings of missionary work. This thought says more than I ever could myself. President Heber J. Grant testified: "I had more joy while in the mission field than ever before or since. Man is that he may have joy, and the joy that I had in the mission field was superior to any I have ever experienced elsewhere." That quote comes from a man who had traveled over the whole world and participated in almost every phase of church service. My heart burns right now as I write this. As I reflect on the joy that has come into my life through missionary service, I cannot imagine not having had those experiences. The only way that you could understand the joy that missionary work brings is to open up your Book of Mormon to Alma 26:11,16 and read what it did for Ammon. Joy, joy beyond description!

Prepare to Serve

Challenge

Listed here are seventeen blessings which Elder Carlos E. Asay one of our General Authorities associated with missionary work during a talk given September 20, 1984, to a prospective Missionary Conference in Provo, Utah. Please go through the list and decide if you could use these items in your own life.

The Blessings of Missionary Service

Blessing	Could You Benefit From This?
• Joy	☐
• Peace of Conscience	☐
• Growth in Knowledge of the Gospel	☐
• Growth in Faith	☐
• Closeness to the Lord	☐
• Companionship of the Holy Spirit	☐
• Growth of Testimony	☐
• Forgiveness of Sins	☐
• Developing and Polishing Character	☐
• Being a Peacemaker	☐
• Rendering Service	☐
• Developing Love and Understanding of People	☐
• Establishing Abiding Friendships	☐
• Memorable Experiences	☐
• Building the Kingdom; Preparing a People for Christ's Second Coming	☐
• Leadership Training	☐
• Eternal Life	☐

Chapter 2

Qualifications for Serving

Belief is the knowledge that we
can do something. It's the inner
feeling that if we undertake, we
can accomplish. For the most part,
all of us have the ability
to look at something and know
whether or not we can do it.
So, in belief there is power:
our eyes are opened; our
opportunities become plain;
our visions become realities.

                         Anonymous

Scriptures:
D & C 4, D & C 18:19, D & C 112:28, D & C 12:8

Elder Stephen
Southern States, Mission

    I remember once, when I was a zone leader near Baton Rouge, La., my companion and I were trying to find a chapel that neither one of us had been to before. It wasn't until we were on the road that we realized that we had each mistakenly assumed that the other knew where we were going. We took the exit off the freeway that led to the town we needed to get to. We took a left at the first stoplight we came to, because it seemed that was where most of the town was. When we came to the next light, I looked at my companion and he looked back at me. "Which way do you think we ought to go?" I asked. "I dunno. What do you think?" was the reply. We discussed it and decided that since we were dedicated servants of the Lord and we were there on important missionary business, we should certainly be entitled to the guidance of the Spirit in this matter. We bowed our heads and said a quick prayer while still there at the stoplight.

"Which way did you feel?"

"Which way did you feel?"

"I think we should go right."

"Yeah, that's what I felt."

Using this process, we made a few more rights and a few more lefts and before we knew it, there we were: lost. We were more lost, in fact, than I think I have ever been. Frustrated at being late for our appointment and perplexed as to why we had not received the inspiration we desired, we decided to head over to the freeway and go back to our original starting point.

We turned left again at the first light and then came to a stop at the light where we had offered our prayer. I looked at my comp and he looked back at me. "Which way do you think we ought to go?" I asked. "I dunno. What do you think?" was the reply. Then, as we looked back up at the stoplight, we saw that, directly across the street, was the very building we had been looking for.

This rather humbling experience taught me a great deal about missionary work. Before we expect any help from God, we should first do all that we can to help ourselves. Sometimes, we try to be so dependant on God that we become blind to our own abilities and the value of our own efforts. Our Heavenly Father is always there to help us, but we must do our part. Sometimes, that simply means opening our eyes.

• • •

What does it take to be a missionary? What do you need to take with you into the mission field besides your new white shirts and your mailman shoes? Do you have a testimony that this is the Lord's work to take with you? Do you feel, strongly, that the gospel message is vital for all men and that it is your personal responsibility to see that others have a chance to hear the message? Added to that testimony do you have knowledge of gospel principles? You can't teach what you don't know. Are you prepared to teach the gospel and testify intelligently of its principles? A missionary must be able to do these things. If you are not prepared, now is the time to change.

In the Church, when we talk about great missionaries, we often think of the four sons of Mosiah. It was said of them that "when they taught, they taught with power and authority of God." How did they become such great missionaries? Were they simply supermen from birth? It doesn't appear so. In fact, they had spent most of their lives in opposition to the Church. We could perhaps learn a great deal by examining how these men developed themselves into such powerful tools for righteousness.

When Alma was reunited with the sons of Mosiah in Zarahemla, he made the following observation:

> *They had searched the scriptures diligently, that they might know the word of God. But this is not all; they had given themselves to much prayer, and fasting; therefore they had the spirit of prophecy, and the spirit of revelation.. (Alma 17:2-3.)*

So we see that the sons of Mosiah weren't just magically transformed into different people when the angel of the Lord appeared to them. All the angel did was to turn them around and instill in them the desire to change. The rest was up to them. It took a tremendous amount of study and prayer and fasting and work to get to the point where they could teach "with power and authority of God." Nothing in life comes easy, but as you can see, miraculous rewards come to those who are willing to pay the price of success. That price is called preparation — whole-hearted preparation. Sure, everybody wants to baptize thousands like the sons of Mosiah, but, as someone once said, more important than the will to win is the will to prepare to win. That's what this book is all about — how you can prepare and develop the qualifications not just of a good missionary, but of a missionary who can teach the gospel truths with "power and authority."

Alma 17:2-3 tells us that the sons of Mosiah "searched the scriptures diligently" and had a firm testimony of the gospel. But if we read in detail of their missionary experiences among the Lamanites, we see other areas of preparation that proved essential to their success. In addition to spiritual and scriptural preparation, the successful missionary must devote time to each of these areas:

1. Mental — The mental challenges of a mission include the ability to effectively plan, to learn the discussions and scriptures, to remember names of hundreds of investigators, members and missionaries, and to perhaps learn a new language and a different set of cultural mores.

2. Social — Just as Ammon gained the respect and trust of King Lamoni, you will have to build relationships of trust with investigators, members and missionaries within your stewardship before you can become effective as a missionary and as a leader.

3. Financial — A mission costs a great deal of money — enough to support you for two years. As a missionary you will have to pay rent, buy food, pay for transportation, clothing, laundry, etc. Once in the mission field, you should never have to worry about money. That is why preparation is so vital.

4. Practical Preparation — You should know how to change a tire, iron a shirt, sew on a button, make your bed, and cook more than just toast.

A missionary prepares in all these areas because he does not want to spend the majority of his time of service just trying to catch up with the other missionaries who came to the mission field prepared. A good missionary prepares in all these areas because he desires to serve a mission that becomes the positive base for the rest of his life.

Prepare to Serve

Challenge

Take a long hard look at how prepared you are to serve. Take a piece of paper and a pencil and actually diagram your levels of preparation. On the sheet of paper make columns for Scriptures, Testimony, Mental, Social, Financial and Practical. Note in each column your strengths and weaknesses in each of these areas. For example, in the practical column, note whether you could prepare your favorite meals. Could you also go to the grocery store and pick out the needed ingredients? If you answered no, then, next to your newly discovered weakness, note what you could do to improve yourself in that area.

Missionary Preparation Checklist:

Area	**Strengths**	**Weaknesses**
Scriptures	_____	_____
Testimony	_____	_____
Mental	_____	_____
Social	_____	_____
Financial	_____	_____
Practical	_____	_____

Chapter 3

Scriptural Preparation

There is an infinite difference between
a little wrong and just right, between
fairly good and the best, between
mediocrity and superiority . . . .

                              Orison Swett Marden

Scriptures:
Alma 37:8-12; D & C 84:54-57,62; 2 Nephi 32:3; 1 Nephi 15:24

Elder Ryan
Colorado, Denver Mission

As a recent convert who was suddenly given two hours a day to study the gospel, I developed a voracious appetite for the scriptures in the early part of my mission. Having grown up in another faith, I was particularly interested in scripturally proving that the switch I had made was the right one. I delighted in discovering new scriptures to substantiate my own religious claims and discredit others. I began to think of myself as quite the hot-shot scriptorian and was getting a little too big for my spiritual breeches. As a relatively new missionary, there was a lot I had to learn about teaching the gospel through the spirit.

In my second area, my companion and I began teaching a young high-school age girl named Cathy. We had been introduced to Cathy by a member of the local ward who went to school with her, and the discussions were going really well. Each of us had felt the spirit many times during the few weeks that we taught her, and she was progressing toward baptism. The only obstacle was her parents, and they proved to be a big one. They were very much against her taking the discussions, and, when we challenged Cathy for baptism, they utterly forbid it. Cathy begged and pleaded, but they refused to listen, and, since she was a minor and still living at home, there was little that could be done. I'm sure her parents felt justified in "saving" their daughter from our weird religion, but Cathy continued to press them. Finally, the parents suggested that Cathy and her two "missionaries" meet with them and their Catholic priest. When I heard this, I was stoked at the chance of "bashing" with a priest one-on-one. Little thought went into the effectiveness of such a meeting on Cathy's conversion or baptism. Indeed, little prayer went into my preparation. All I could think about was the priest and the inevitable glory I would receive by confounding him.

When the appointed day arrived, I was swelled with anticipation. We arrived at the Catholic church and were directed to the priest's office, where Cathy and her parents were waiting. As the discussion began, the first thing the priest hit us with was the old "you-guys-believe-you-can-become-gods" attack. Amused at his lack of originality, I was elated at the facileness of this first offensive. I masterfully parried with an appeal to scripture. Though I had my own scriptures with me, I asked the priest if I might borrow his for a moment. In his own Bible, I flipped to one of the standard missionary scriptures in Hebrews 1:1-3. I pointed out the part in verse 2 where is reads that God appointed his Son "heir of all things," and I asked the priest what he thought that meant. He replied that it meant simply that Jesus Christ inherited all that God has. I then asked if inheriting all that God has qualified Jesus Christ to be called a god, and the priest impatiently replied that he could not see what I was getting at, since he and his faith already believed that Jesus Christ was a god because he did inherit all that his Father had. What did all this have to do with his original challenge? I then asked him if he wouldn't mind turning back a few pages in his Bible and reading Roman's 8:16-17. I watched his countenance fall to the floor as he read aloud the words "The spirit itself beareth witness with our spirit, that we are the children of God: and if children, then heirs; heirs of God, and joint-heirs with Christ." While I was gloating triumphantly, the priest pulled a maneuver that I have since found to be typical for an anti-mormon who has been confounded on a point of doctrine; he just brushed it aside and switched to another point. Robbed of my precious victory! He was not interested in proving that he was right, just in proving that we were wrong.

His next plan of attack was more indirect. He accused us of belonging to an occult religion. This had been a recurrent theme during our discussions with Cathy, as her parents had evidently been coached by their priest in giving her objections to present to us. They had always been easy objections to overcome because they weren't really Cathy's objections, but now we were being forced to deal with it directly.

I was having a tough time with this one. I was used to the church being called a cult, but not "occult." What made it even more difficult was that I wasn't completely sure what the word meant. I knew it had something to do with mysterious things, so I decided to use this as my first line of defense. Recalling some of my own early education in a Catholic school, I asked the priest if it wasn't true that one of the most basic creeds of his religion was The Creed of St. Athanasius. He replied that it was. I then asked him if that creed was more commonly known as the "great, incomprehensible mystery," because of its reference to the Trinity as "The Father incomprehensible, the Son incomprehensible, and the Holy Ghost incomprehensible." Getting impatient, he replied that yes, that was also correct. My next question was, "So, at the foundation of your church is a creed that you call the great, incomprehensible mystery?" He said, "Yes, but you are avoiding the accusation against you. What does any of this have to do with my original point?" I asked him if I could look at the dictionary that was on the bookshelf behind him. When he gave it to me, I looked up the word occult and read the definition out loud: "A mystery; That which is not able to be understood." I looked up and asked, "Now which one of our churches sounds like it is occult?"

Prepare to Serve

After this, I felt like getting up and strutting around the room. I half expected to not only baptize Cathy, but also her family and the priest. As it turned out, though, we didn't get a single baptism out of it. Not even Cathy. All I had done was exercise my vanity and invite the spirit of contention. I had excluded the Holy Ghost from the entire discussion. I learned the hard way that without the Spirit "you shall not teach," and that we were sent out to convert, not convince. This was a heartbreaking lesson for me.

Many months later, in another area with another companion, I found myself teaching a family who had become as dear to me as anyone else I had taught on my mission. The entire family was progressing towards baptism. We shared many choice, sacred experiences as they progressed through the discussions. Each of us had been moved to tears at various times as the Spirit bore witness of the Gospel and of our love for one another. During the week prior to their scheduled baptism, we arranged to meet with them almost daily. On one evening, we had planned to show them one of the Church movies from the ward library. The moment we walked in the door, though, we could sense that something was terribly wrong. As we went into the living room where the family was gathered, we saw two other people who we had never seen before. The introductions were coldly made, and we learned that the two were somewhat prominent anti-Mormons. One of them was a minister of another faith who had written an anti-Mormon book.

My heart sank as I thought of the possibility of losing this precious family. My warrior's spirit rose to the occasion, though, and I could feel the hairs begin to rise on my back as I listened to a venom-filled tirade in which this minister defamed the Church and its prophets. As I opened my mouth to respond, though, my great companion placed his hand on my knee and spoke before me. However, instead of directing his comments to the two antagonists, he turned to the family, who were sitting on the couch across from us. To them he quietly said, "Do you remember the way we have felt these last few weeks as we have been discussing the Gospel? Do you remember the feelings that we identified as the Holy Ghost and the times we were all moved to tears?

Prepare to Serve

Do you remember how you said you felt last week after praying about baptism and about the Book of Mormon?" They all quietly but firmly nodded their heads. My companion then asked, "And how have you felt tonight as you've listened to these men speak?" I could see in their eyes that they were feeling the same way I was — dark and dirty. "What does that tell you about what these men have been saying?" my companion asked.

Nothing more needed to be said. The father of the family stood up and asked the two men to leave. My wonderful companion had not only frustrated the efforts of these anti-Mormons, but had, at the same time, significantly strengthened the testimonies of the family. What was amazing was that he really hadn't said anything. He offered no rebuttals and defended no doctrine. He simply asked questions of the family that led them to realize something they already knew to be true — that the Holy Ghost had borne witness of our message of the restored Gospel, and therefore the message must be true. I learned that no amount of knowledge or ability can compensate for an absence of the Spirit. The family was baptized as scheduled that weekend.

• • •

The Jensen family is pure gold. You and your companion met them at the home of the Hahn family during a special family home evening. They weren't interested in your message at first, but they became more serious as the talk moved to the plan of salvation. During the family home evening, their interest deepened, yet they declined an invitation for a later discussion. However, the next day Mr. Jensen called Brother Hahn at work and said they would like to learn more about the gospel. For the last six weeks you and your companion have seen the Jensens three or four times per week. You've taught them the basic discussions and they have come to Church three of the last four Sundays.

The Hahns and the rest of the branch have been very receptive to the Jensens. During this time you have come to care quite a bit for Mr. and Mrs.

Jensen and their two children, Jan and Michael. After much prayer and discussion, you and your companion have decided that the time has come to challenge them to be baptized. Tonight was to be the night.

But when you arrived you found that the minister from the Jensens' present church had invited himself to participate in the evening's discussion. Though you are less than thrilled with his presence, it is obvious to you that he has a good relationship with the Jensens. The minister has conveniently brought with him a list of questions about LDS beliefs, including new revelation, apostles and prophets, baptism by immersion, etc. You try to answer his questions by relying on the Spirit, but he insists that you support your answers with evidence from the Bible.

Are you prepared to answer his questions?

If you have paid attention to the scriptures you have been asked to study and have reviewed and discussed them in their historical and spiritual context, then you can use the Bible quite effectively to support the truths of the gospel. And if you can speak authoritatively about the Bible and the ancient Church, then the Spirit can effectively use you to teach and bear witness of the truths of the Gospel.

If you haven't studied and pondered the events in the Bible and the Book of Mormon, then all you can do is parrot some answers you may have heard from others. Or you may spend your time looking up scriptures in your Bible's topical guide (which is a great place to look for answers, but not when you are on the spot).

Once again, preparation will prove the key to your success. Remember — study, ponder and pray. Then when the pressure is on, you can deal with it. I am not suggesting that the Jensens will fall through the cracks if you cannot answer all of their minister's questions. But you are much more likely to influence the Jensens and their minister if you can teach with power and authority as did the sons of Mosiah.

You might be saying, "But that was thousands of years ago. The sons of Mosiah aren't like us today; they were special." Let me tell you, the sons of Mosiah were boys who were called upon to serve. If you had lived then, you could have just as easily been one of them. Their secret was the power with which they operated. And how did they get their power and authority? You guessed it — through diligent study, prayer, and fasting, or in other words — preparation.

Consider what the Lord says about the importance of study:

Seek not to declare my word, but first seek to obtain my word, and then shall your tongue be loosed; then, if you desire, you shall have my Spirit and my word, yea, the power of God unto the convincing of men.

But now hold your peace; study my word which hath gone forth among the children of men, and also study my word which shall come forth among the children of men, or that which is now translating, yea, until you have obtained all which I shall grant unto the children of men in this generation, and then shall all things be added thereto. (D&C 11:21-22.)

Notice that the Lord said to Hyrum Smith to "seek first to obtain [His] word" before attempting to preach it. Notice how He told Hyrum to "study" ALL of His word that was available and then the Lord would grant him His Spirit and the power of convincing men.

The Lord is not going to personally reveal the truths contained in the scriptures to you every time an investigator asks a tough question (as convenient as that would be). But if you will study the scriptures and pray about them, then He will reveal to you what you should say and which scriptures you should use to answer investigators' (or their minister's) questions.

When I served as a missionary one of my biggest fears was that I would not be able to remember a scripture or something that I had read. After all, there are hundreds and hundreds of pages and items to learn . . . Please consider what the Lord says in D & C 84:85: "Neither take ye thought for beforehand, what ye shall say; but treasure up in your minds continually the words of life, and it shall be given you in that very hour that portion that shall be meted unto every man."

Here again the Lord asks us to prepare by treasuring up in our minds, or in other words, pondering, the truths of the scriptures. And again, if we will do so He promises that in our hour of need He will give unto us what we shall say. So we need not fear — if we are prepared.

When the Lord says "Treasure up in your minds continually the words of life, and it shall be given you in the very hour that portion that shall be meted unto every man", it is a promise that I know is true. During the two years of my mission in Sweden I personally experienced dozens of times what the Lord describes with the words, "it shall be given you in the very hour . . . ." I also experienced the pain that comes from not being able to teach with power.

During the early part of my mission in Sweden I had became extremely busy with my reports, and the other busywork aspects of missionary life. I was reading my scriptures every day, but not with the diligence I should have. Many times, I would put off my scripture study until right when I got into bed. I can't say that I ever woke up with the scriptures still in my hands, but quite often I don't think I could remember one word that I had read five minutes earlier. I was just going through the motions and passing my eyes over the required pages.

During one teaching opportunity with a young man, I was called upon to answer a question that I could have shot off a quick answer to, but I knew that I should use the Bible to illustrate the answer. When my mind came up blank as to where the scripture was, I fully expected the Lord to help me find the right scripture to use like he had so many times before. So I reached for my Bible, thumbed it open, and waited expectantly for the help I had so gotten used to. Instead of answers, my mind was filled with an image of the way I had been studying the scriptures. I saw myself just running my eyes over the words. During seconds which seemed like minutes, I was chastised like never before. I had not been treasuring up the scriptures in my mind.

Prepare to Serve

That moment passed; I still couldn't think of the scripture, so I attempted to describe what the scripture I couldn't find said, and what it meant in the context of his question. My soul ached; I knew I wasn't prepared and that I hadn't done my part.

An important part of your preparation is to study and become familiar with the scriptures and to gain a firm testimony of them. Using the scriptures can support and clarify points of doctrine and can bring the Spirit into a discussion. You will find that it is the scriptures (more specifically, the Book of Mormon) that convert. Many people, including one of my heroes, Parley P. Pratt, have been converted almost entirely through contact with the Book of Mormon. You must learn to use the Book of Mormon. It is the only tangible aspect of the gospel that you can leave in an investigator's hands after teaching them for the first time. President Benson has stressed the need for more and better prepared missionaries who know the Book of Mormon. "This is a day of preparation. We need missionaries to match our message. Those missionaries who use it know that the Book of Mormon is the instrument to convince the hearts of men. There is a difference between those converts who are built on the gospel and the Book of Mormon and those who are not."

The Bible will also be a very important tool on your mission. Investigators will often insist that you support your claims with scriptures from the Bible and not the Book of Mormon. Though not often read, the Bible possesses an unquestioned sanctity for most Christians. A well-prepared missionary should know how to locate Biblical scriptures that support the principles presented in the discussions. The discussions give a list of scriptural resources with each principle. Make sure to take note of those scriptures that are taken from the Bible. For example, when teaching the discussion on eternal progression, there are several scriptural resources listed for the principle of our pre-mortal existence. If an investigator is having a difficult time accepting the idea of a pre-existence and wants to know if there is anywhere in the Bible that talks about it, you can show him Jeremiah 1:5. I can remember teaching a man and trying to explain to him that the resurrection would be universal, that all men would be resurrected regardless of their deeds. The first scriptures I used with him were a couple of excellent scriptures in the book of Alma dealing with the resurrection. When he insisted that this was strictly a Mormon concept, I had him turn in his Bible to I Corinthians 15:21-22 and John 5:28-29. Through the use of the Bible as a companion text to the Book of Mormon, this man came to realize that the resurrection as Christ's free gift was indeed an eternal principle.

> *The scriptures testify of God and contain the words of eternal life. They become the burden of [a missionary's] message — even the tools of your trade. Your confidence will be directly related to your knowledge of God's word."* (Elder Thomas S. Monson, *In Conference Report,* Oct. 1969, p. 93.)

At no other time in your life will you have the marvelous opportunity of devoting two hours each day to studying the Gospel. After your mission, life moves so fast and has so many demands that it takes a great deal of discipline to maintain any kind of a regular scripture study schedule, and even then, it will rarely be for more than thirty minutes a day. As a missionary, you have two hours already scheduled into each and every day. Take advantage of this great opportunity. To help you study effectively and in an organized way, you will use the missionary gospel study program. This booklet is a tremendous tool. It divides missionary gospel study into two parts: 1) individual study, and 2) companion study.

One hour every day will be spent in individual gospel study. This hour is divided into three areas of study:

1. Thirty minutes daily Book of Mormon reading
2. Reading in other standard works
3. Study of the Gospel by topics

The individual study schedule is divided into fifty-two weeks. Each day you should study the Book of Mormon for thirty minutes. A chart is provided to record your progress. In addition, there is a weekly assignment given in the other standard works. For example, in Week 1 (the first week in January) you will read Matthew 1-12. The next week, you are

Prepare to Serve

---

assigned Matthew 13-23, and so forth. By reading about three pages a day, you will have read the New Testament, the Doctrine and Covenants, the Pearl of Great Price and most of the Old Testament within a year. Now that's an accomplishment to get excited about. The schedule also gives you a different Gospel topic to study each week. The topics correspond to the principles presented in the discussions. You are given a study outline for each topic which lists scripture references, study questions and other sources of information. By taking some notes of what you learn about each topic and then organizing them for future reference, you'll be set for Sacrament talks and Relief Society/Priesthood lessons for the rest of your life.

You will also study with your companion for an hour each day. During this time, you will discuss what you've been learning about the topic of the week. You should share ideas and scriptures and answer questions together about the topic. You will also study the discussions and the Missionary Guide during this hour. If your mission requires you to speak a foreign language, you will spend an additional thirty minutes practicing and studying the language.

You can obtain a copy of the Missionary Gospel Study Program by contacting your ward or stake mission leader.

To supplement your studies, you will need to bring several books with you into the mission field. The recommended missionary library includes the following books:

1. *The LDS Editions of the Standard Works* (including the Topical Guide)
2. *A Marvelous Work and a Wonder*
3. *Jesus the Christ*
4. *Gospel Principles* (PBIC0245)
5. *Truth Restored* (PBMI1064)
6. *The Articles of Faith*

Prepare to Serve

One of the great blessings of a mission is the closeness a missionary develops to the Savior and the strengths that he acquires through searching and understanding the scriptures. Friends and family of returning missionaries comment on how much they have grown spiritually and how much they have learned. Take advantage of the opportunity before you. If you don't, you will always have regrets and wonder about the person you might have become. As a missionary friend of mine used to say, "If you work on your mission, your mission will work on you."

You will discover that there is a big difference between reading the scriptures and studying them. You can read the scriptures for two hours per day with hardly a word sinking in, or you can spend two hours pondering, discussing, and enjoying just one small chapter. You will find that if you will pause in your scripture study and ponder the events, imagining the people and circumstances as they actually happened, then the scriptures will take on a new life and vitality.

But what about reading scriptures before your mission? It should be obvious by now that missionaries should have read all of the standard works before embarking on their missions. President Ezra Taft Benson has given renewed emphasis to study of the Book of Mormon. He has said that it is our most important teaching tool. (Ensign, April 1987) As President Monson said, the scriptures are the tools of missionary work. If you will read them all before your mission (yes, it is possible) and ponder them as you go, then you will be prepared to use these tools.

When I first went on my own mission, I was constantly haunted by a shadow called insecurity. Everyone else knew so much about the scriptures. When I taught, I actually found myself dreading questions which would require an encyclopedic knowledge of the scriptures. My own personal problem was solved by an inspired district leader who encouraged me to begin not only reading the scriptures but studying them. I have a testimony of the importance of scripture study. When you study the scriptures, they become more than just words. They become thoughts and concepts which you can not only express to others but can begin to more fully live by. The sweet feeling of understanding and testimony is an unspoken method of communication to those who you teach. Scriptural understanding will greatly increase your ability to teach effectively.

Now, let's go back to the Jensen's living room. You have followed the advice of your leaders and the suggestions in this book and have studied the scriptures (including the Bible) and pondered and prayed concerning what you have read. Following the Spirit you are able to refer the Jensen's minister to several scriptures that support our beliefs. You speak softly, yet firmly and with a quiet dignity and authority that one does not usually expect from one so young. Indeed, the minister is inwardly astounded (as are you). But outwardly he has to save face. He can't give up and begins to ask more questions. Here the Spirit tells you to politely decline to continue answering his questions at this time. You humbly bear testimony of continuing revelation and change the subject, thus avoiding an unpleasant and fruitless "Bible bash."

Even though religious arguments can be a good release to "prove how much you know and how right we are," there is not power of testimony and conversion in heated conversations. Avoid "Bible Bashing." Teach with the spirit. Change the conversation to personal testimony, revelation, and the basics of the gospel. Operate with the spirit and love.

Challenge

Set a goal and outline a plan for yourself to have read the scriptures completely before you leave on your mission. If you are reading this the night before you leave, that may not be realistic. But, don't ignore the challenge. Make it a point to have completed the entire scriptures during the next few months. You are going to need that knowledge and power to teach effectively.

Chapter 4

Spiritual Preparation

There are those who travel and those
who are going somewhere. They are
different and yet they are the same.
The success has this over his rivals:
he knows where he is going.

                      Mark Caine

Scriptures:
D & C 50:13-29; D & C 84:61; Alma 5:45-46; Gal. 5:22-23;
D & C 100:7-8

Elder Joe
Washington, Seattle Mission

My mission provided me with many opportunities to use and witness the power of the priesthood. In addition to baptisms and priesthood leadership, I was also able to exercise the priesthood in giving many blessings to the sick. In my first area my companion and I regularly stopped by the hospital to check the clergy register to see if anyone had checked in as LDS. Because of the area we were in, the hospital quite often admitted patients who were flown in by helicopter from remote, outlying areas. If any of these patients happened to be LDS, chances are that none of the local ward members would know about them.

Prepare to Serve

On one occasion, we were able to administer to a man who had been involved in a rather serious industrial accident on one of the offshore operations and had been flown in to the hospital. As we entered his room we noticed an old man in the bed next to him who looked like he was in really bad shape. My companion asked the nurse what was wrong with the old man, and she replied that, among other things, he had been stricken with a case of cancer that his body was too weak to fight off. The way he looked, I wouldn't have been surprised if he had gone the way of all the earth while we were right there in the room. Anyway, we gave the blessing to the accident victim and stayed a few minutes trying to comfort the family. We were on our way out when, as we passed the old man's bed, he very softly called for our attention. We went over to his bedside, and he asked if we would do to him what we had done to the other guy. We explained that we were Mormons and that it was kind of a Mormon thing that we had done but that we would be more than happy to do it to him. At his request, we then anointed and blessed him. With shame, I remember thinking as we walked out of the hospital that, given the shape the old man was in, we had probably just wasted some good oil.

Some three months later, having long since forgotten the old man in the hospital room, I had taken my new companion to a local rest home to "preach" one Sunday afternoon. We had been conducting these Sunday worship services once a month for as long as I had been in the area. We did it more as a community service than for any hope of conversions, and, consequently, we kept the services very basic and nondenominational. On this particular Sunday, one of the aides approached us and asked if we were aware that there was a Mormon living at the rest home. When we said no, she pointed him out to us. Sitting in a wheelchair across the room was the old man from the hospital! You could have bowled me over with a feather. We went over to talk to him, and when we said that we didn't know he was a Mormon, he said, "Well, I'm not really. It's just that when I checked into this place, they asked me what religion I was and I couldn't think of any other religion that I would rather claim. After you fellows left the hospital that day, I started recovering. It shocked the doctors as much as it did me. I think they had already promised my room to someone else. When I became well enough, I came here because I didn't have any family around to take care of me."

I was stunned. My companion quickly picked up the conversation and informed the man, whose name we learned was Francis, that we would be more than happy to come back and tell him more about our church. We set up an appointment to begin teaching him, and what followed was some of the most spiritual teaching moments of my mission. We baptized 67-year-old Francis a few weeks later. I still remember our first discussion with him, when we taught him the steps to prayer and had him offer the closing prayer. He looked up from his prayer and began crying. "I've lived sixty-seven years and you boys have just taught me how to say my first prayer," he said.

I was soon transferred, but Francis continued to progress in the Gospel. Ward members came to the rest home to read the Book of Mormon to him, and he was ordained to the priesthood. I got busy in my mission and eventually lost contact with the people of my first area. Though I drew great strength from their memory, a missionary's work is always in front of him, and there was much to be done.

My mission took me many places and brought many more special people into my life. For the last few months, I served as assistant to the President. It was during this period that several circumstances combined and I found myself reunited for one evening with my old companion from my first area. He and I were alone in the mission office on a Saturday evening while I worked on some paperwork that needed my attention. We received a phone call from one of the major hospitals in the city, informing us that a patient there had requested that some Mormon elders come to give him a blessing. It was not unusual for the mission office to get such requests. We usually sent the office elders or the missionaries whose area it was. Since we were there alone, we decided just to go do it ourselves. When we arrived at the hospital and walked into the room, who did we find lying on the bed but Francis. Now, keep in mind that we were six and a half hours away from the town where we originally met and baptized Francis and it had been almost a year and a half since we had last seen him. Also realize that my companion and myself, the same two missionaries who had given him his first blessing and had taught and baptized him, were together that night by "accident" for the first time since that first area. No seas were parted and nobody walked on any water, but you can't convince Francis that, as we walked through that hospital room door, the most incredible miracle in the world hadn't just occurred.

I thank my Father in Heaven for the Holy Priesthood, for missions and for the Church. I am humbled at having been given the opportunity to be a small part of it all. I know that this is a gospel of miracles, both great and small. I know that the gospel changes lives.

• • •

Scripture study involves more than just reading through the standard works. It also includes pondering and meditating upon the things you are reading. To ponder is to think deeply and to pray.

As mentioned in Chapter 3, scripture study involves much more than just reading in the standard works. It also means contemplating the people and events and considering how their actions might relate to you and the people you teach. As you consider the events in the scriptures, take time to talk with your Father in Heaven about them. There is a reason He considers them so important. Don't be bashful to ask Him about them. That is how He intends for you to learn. I promise it will work.

Those who pray earnestly are rewarded with great spiritual blessings. Try talking earnestly with your Father in Heaven about the events you are studying. After a few weeks, ask yourself if your understanding has increased. I think you will be surprised at the people, events and principles you have come to know. You will find that ever so gradually, drop-by-drop, your Heavenly Father has begun to fill the cup of your spiritual knowledge. And you will realize that you, yes, you, have been receiving personal revelation. And you will also realize that this revelation didn't come in some dramatic fashion, but rather that it distilled upon your mind as the dews of heaven.

This is personal revelation.

Consider how the following people grew in understanding through pondering the scriptures and praying about them:

Moroni 10:3
Moroni exhorted future readers of writings of ancient American prophets to ponder the scriptures in their hearts. If they would do so and pray about them sincerely, he said, they could come to know of their truth, indeed even the truth of all things.

3 Nephi 17:2-3
The Savior, when He appeared to the Nephites in ancient America, admonished the spiritually weak Nephites to return to their homes and ponder upon the things which He had taught that day. He also admonished them to ask His Father In Heaven to help them understand His words.

1 Nephi 11:1
Nephi listened to his father recount a vision he had received and was filled with a desire to know what his father had seen. As Nephi sat pondering his father's words, he got his wish and was caught up in a vision.

D&C 138:1
It was while President Joseph F. Smith was pondering over the scriptures that he received a vision concerning the preaching of the gospel to the spirits in prison.

The more time you spend considering the things of the spirit the more time the Holy Ghost will have to bear witness to you of their truth. That is why pondering is so important because it invites the presence of the Spirit. Soon you will recognize how the Spirit speaks to you.

Prepare to Serve

God's truth can only be known through the Spirit of the Lord. This is the only way anyone can understand the Gospel. Yet the humblest servant of God can know the truth through the Spirit. You have learned to "say your prayers."

- Do you pray often, "with real intent," talking with the Lord thoughtfully and humbly and gratefully?
- Do you acknowledge your faults and troubles to him and then seek to increase your faith and overcome your weaknesses?
- Do you attend your meetings regularly? Do you practice controlling your mind while there, being prayerful, meditating?
- When you partake of the Sacrament of the Lord's Supper, are you worshipping?
- Do you support your bishop and all others who lead?
- Do you really love your Heavenly Father and his Holy Son? Do you truly try to serve him and keep his commandments?

Finally, your study, prayer, and meditation will bring you the greatest satisfaction if you will fast regularly. Fasting is a sacrifice that brings forth great blessings from heaven. As you set aside the needs of the body for a day and concentrate on the needs of the spirit, you will obtain increased spiritual strength and discernment. Consider how fasting brought strength and wisdom to the following people:

Alma fasted for many days before he met Amulek who was to greatly assist him in his ministry (Alma 5:45-46).

The Savior fasted for forty days before He began His public ministry.

While fasting is an essential ingredient of your spiritual development you should not fast too often. Missionaries are generally encouraged to fast only once a month and for only twenty-four hours. Sincerity in fasting is more important than excessive frequency or length.

Consider these formulas for spirituality:

Moroni 10:4-5
Moroni testifies that if we will ask with a sincere heart, with faith in Christ, and with real intent, then we can know the Book of Mormon is true and can know the truth of all things.

Alma 5:45-46
Alma fasted and prayed "many days" to know for himself that Jesus was the Christ and that the teachings of the prophets WHICH HE HAD STUDIED were true.

Matthew 17:14-21
The Lord's disciples failed to cast a devil out of a man. When they asked the Master why, he told them that they needed faith and that difficult miracles could only be accomplished through much fasting and prayer.

D & C 19:38
In the Doctrine and Covenants the Lord promised Martin Harris that continual prayer would bring a blessing greater than the treasures of the earth.

Joseph F. Smith said this about prayer:

I pray you, my young brethren . . . who are liable to be called to preach the gospel to the world, when you are called to go out, I pray that you will know how to approach God in prayer. It is not such a difficult thing to learn how to pray.

It is not the words we use particularly that constitute prayer . . . . True, faithful, earnest prayer consists more in the feeling that rises from the heart and from the inward desire of our spirits to supplicate the Lord in humility and in faith, that we may receive his blessings. It matters not how simple the words may be, if our desires are genuine and we come before the Lord with a broken heart and contrite spirit to ask him for that which we need.
(Joseph F. Smith, *Gospel Doctrine*, 5th ed., Salt Lake City: Deseret Book Company, 1939, p. 219.)

Prepare to Serve

When we think of fasting we think of testimony meeting, donations, and growling stomachs, bad breath in Church meetings and a race home to the refrigerator after Church. Fasting in the true sense is much more than that. It is a cleansing that, when used in coordination with your mission rules, can channel your efforts and, like a magnifying glass focuses the rays of the sun, when combined with purpose and prayer can directly call upon the spirit to assist you in your missionary efforts.

One particularly moving experience on my mission was when, as a young District Leader, I was called upon to work with an Elder who wanted to go home from his mission. He was a little homesick and really hadn't got caught up in the missionary spirit. Before this Elder and I went out I talked with him about joining me in a special fast. The day before we went out we began the fast with a prayer with a purpose. We specifically asked that the Lord bless him with an understanding of the importance of his missionary efforts. The next day we began our efforts with another prayer and out we went. I can't say that during that day we ran into crowds of Swedes waiting in the streets to join the Church, but I can say this: That day we talked about the Church and in the back of a subway car bore testimonies of the gospel to each other. We talked about our families and of our desires to grow in the gospel. We worked hard that day. As the day drew to an end, this Elder asked me if we could get off the subway and do just a little more tracting. As we got off we both started to walk down the street. We stopped at an intersection and thought for a minute, then without a word we went around the corner, up another street, and went into an apartment building and climbed up to the top floor. There we were faced with two doors. Still, without a word of discussion, we turned and knocked on a door which bore a Polish name. As the door opened, we were greeted by a fantastic family. We introduced ourselves, and they let us in. We taught the first discussion that night to them and challenged them to read the Book of Mormon that we loaned them. They said they would. As we left, tears filled our eyes as we thanked the Lord for His blessings that day. I followed this family's progress for several weeks until I was transferred and was later thrilled to hear that they soon were baptized as members in the Church.

We could have just tracted that day and rationalized about how embarrassed he would be if he went home early. Instead, we fasted, bore our testimonies to each other, and answered the promptings of the Spirit which led us to the door of a family which was ready for the Gospel message. The Lord's plan is clear. His blessings will surely follow.

President Spencer W. Kimball has asked that all members of the Church include in their prayers a plea that the Lord will soften the hearts of leaders of nations and open doors throughout the world to the preaching of the gospel. **Full-time missionaries should remember to make this request in their prayers.**

So, what can you, as a prospective missionary, do?

Here you are with several months to go before you can submit your missionary papers. President Kimball's words stick in your mind. You recognize that they belong to you. Try this assignment. You can start right now. Kneel down and pray that the Lord will open the doors of the nations so that His missionaries can enter and teach the gospel.

Go ahead, — ask.

You can do so with a clear conscience since you are preparing yourself to teach the gospel. Do this for several days — you have to give it time. After a week has passed, ask yourself, "What has happened to me? Do I feel any different? How do I feel about missionary work?" You will find, as you sincerely pray for doors to be opened, that your desire to share the gospel will increase. And coupled with that desire to share the gospel will come a desire to prepare for the great work in which you are about to be engaged.

As you pray for the missionary efforts, this would also be a good time to evaluate your personal prayers in general. As a matter of fact, why not write down an actual evaluation of your prayers?

Write down some quantitative facts first. For example:

- How often do you pray each day?
- How long is each prayer?
- What time of day do you pray?
- Which prayer is the longest?
- Which is the shortest?

Next record your impressions of your prayers' overall quality. For example, do you frequently use vain repetitions such as "I thank you for this day," or "Bless all the needy", "Help me to be better," etc.

- Are your prayers more spontaneous at different times of the day?
- Does your mind wander?
- Do you feel as if someone is really listening?
- How long do you listen after each prayer?
- When and how do you receive answers to your prayers?
- When do you feel the most uplifted?

Next, ask, "How can I improve?" As you evaluate the quantity and quality of your prayers, you will find areas where you are deficient. After consideration map solutions which you tailor to fit each problem area.

One of the best ways to improve the quality of your prayers is begin speaking to your Father in Heaven as if He were right there in your room. Learn to talk with Him as if He were your best friend and closest confidant. Remember, He issued the invitation to come unto Him and it was He who said "Draw near unto me and I will draw near unto you" (D&C 88:63).

Learn to talk openly and sincerely with your Father in Heaven and you will kneel down with greater enthusiasm and leave encouraged and edified.

There are other important factors that will affect your spiritual well-being. For example, what are your motives for serving a mission?

Prepare to Serve

Brigham Young, our second prophet said, "If you go on a mission to preach the Gospel with lightness and frivolity in your hearts, looking for this and that, and to learn what is in the world, and not having your minds riveted... on the cross of Christ, you will go and return in vain... Let your minds be centered on your missions."

Having the proper motives for serving a mission is essential to spiritual preparation. Are you entering the mission field because your Father in Heaven needs you? Or are you going in order to please your parents, friends, bishop, boyfriend, or girlfriend? If it is for one of the latter reasons, then you are certainly not the first person to go on a mission with those motives. But wait a moment. Think about what you are doing. Don't you want your mission to be willful service motivated by love for your Heavenly Father? I don't want you to get hung up on this, but the right motives are very important. Since you have by now begun to feel confident about your prayers, you can ask Heavenly Father to help you obtain the desire to serve that is your desire, not someone else's. After all, it is your mission, not your parents', bishop's, children's, boyfriend's or girlfriend's.

The angel Moroni told Joseph Smith that he "must have no other object in view in getting the plates but *to glorify God*, and must not be influenced by any other motive than that of *building his kingdom*; otherwise I could not get them." (JS-H 1:46; italics added.) Moroni's warning also applies to missionary work. The missionary who serves because of his love for God, mankind and to build the kingdom will be blessed. A missionary who serves because his Dad has promised him a new car will get just that at the end of two years of motion.

President Ezra Taft Benson on his mission to England not only learned the principle of dedication, but also how obedience brings great blessings in missionary service.

> *Let me talk about obedience. You're learning now to keep all the commandments of the Lord. As you do so, you will have His Spirit to be with you. You'll feel good about yourselves. You can't do wrong and feel right. It's impossible! One of the great lessons I*

learned on my first mission was the principle of total obedience. In 1923 I was serving a mission in Great Britain. At that time there was great opposition to the Church. It began with the ministers and then spread through the press. Many anti-Mormon articles appeared in the daily press. A number of anti-Mormon movies were shown, and derogatory plays were produced on the stage. The general theme was the same—that Mormon missionaries were in England to lure away British girls and make slaves of them on Utah farms. Today that seems fantastic, but in those days it was very real. In some places we even had to stop tracting because of such misunderstandings.

One time we received a letter from mission headquarters instructing us that we should discontinue all street meetings. At that time I was serving as the conference president, and my companion was the conference clerk. When this instruction arrived, we already had a meeting scheduled for the following Sunday night. So we reasoned that we would hold that meeting and then discontinue street meetings thereafter. That's where we made our mistake!

The next Sunday evening we held our street meeting down near the railway station as scheduled. The crowd was large and unruly. In our efforts to preach to them, my companion and I stood back to back. He spoke in one direction, and I faced the other half of the crowd.

When the saloons closed, the rougher, coarser element came out on the streets, many under the influence of liquor. The crowd became noisy, and those on the outside were not able to hear too well.

Some yelled, "What's the excitement?" Others yelled back, "It's those dreadful Mormons." To this, others responded, "Let's get them and throw them in the river."

Soon an attempt was made to trample us under their feet. But since we were taller than the average man there, we put our hands on their shoulders and prevented them from getting us under their feet. During the excitement, my companion and I became separated. They took him down from the far side of the railway station and me down the near side. Things began to look pretty bad. Then a big husky fellow came up to me as some of the others formed a circle around me about ten feet in diameter. The man looked me straight in the eye and said, "Young man, I believe every word you said tonight.!"

By this time a British policeman had worked his way through the crowd. He took me by the arm and said, "Young man, you come with me. You're lucky to be alive in this crowd." He led me several blocks and then ordered, "Now you get to your lodge and don't come out anymore tonight."

When I arrived at the lodge, I found that my companion was not yet there. I worried and then prayed and waited. I became so concerned about him that I decided to disguise my appearance by putting on an old American cap and taking off my topcoat. Then I went out to try to find him.

As I neared the place of the meeting, a man recognized me and asked, "Have you seen your companion?"

I said, "No. Where is he?"

He responded, "He's down on the other side of the railway station with one side of his head mashed in." This frightened me greatly, and I sprinted to the site as fast as I could. Before I reached the railway station, however, I met the same policeman again. He said, "I thought I told you to stay in and not come out on the street again tonight."

I replied, "You did, officer. But I'm concerned about my companion. Do you know where he is?" He replied, "Yes, he got a nasty blow on the side of his head, but he's gone to the lodge now. I walked partway with him as I did earlier with you. Now you get back there and don't come out anymore tonight."

So I went back to the lodge and found my companion disguising himself in order to go out and look for me. We threw our arms around each other and knelt together in prayer. From that experience I learned always to follow counsel, and that lesson has followed me all the days of my life.

Moral Preparation

Moral cleanliness will be the base for all of your dealings with God and others on your mission. Moral preparation means that you are honest, live the Word of Wisdom and the law of chastity, and repent of serious transgressions.

Consider the following scriptures:

D & C 121:45
The Lord admonishes us through Joseph Smith to let virtue garnish our thoughts unceasingly and then doctrines of the kingdom will distill upon us as the dews from heaven.

D & C 89:19, 20
The Lord promises us if we will obey the Word of Wisdom we will run and not be weary and walk and not faint and will find great treasures of knowledge.

D & C 38:42
The Lord tells the Church to go out from among the wicked and to be clean.

D & C 88:88
The Lord admonishes his followers to not become entangled in sins and thereby to remain free.

Prepare to Serve

D & C 58:42, 43
The Lord tells a gathering of His saints to repent of their sins by confessing them and forsaking them and that if they would do so, He would forgive them.

As previously mentioned, you will have more than one interview with your bishop before being recommended to serve. Your bishop ensures that you are physically and financially capable of serving a mission. If you have physical or financial limitations, he will be able to help you get the proper assistance. It is also the bishop's role to determine your moral worthiness. This is a time for you to be frank and discuss any problems you may have that could affect your worthiness to serve. Your bishop should be able to give you counsel and instructions so that you correct any problems and leave them firmly behind you.

Ask yourself the following questions to assess your worthiness:

- Do you understand what it means to be morally clean?
- Are you morally clean?
- Have you ever been guilty of conduct which you understand to be immoral or improper or questionable? If so, have you followed the program of the Lord in making things right?
- Do you understand the principles of repentance?
- Have you been honest and honorable in your relationships with others?
- Do you respect, honor, and obey the law?
- Are you thoroughly converted to the Word of Wisdom?
- Are you living it conscientiously? Happily?
- Are you dependable? Is your word important to you?
- Do you keep your promises?

If you are not satisfied with any of your answers, if you are not worthy, now is the time to get yourself ready. It is much easier to do your repenting before you enter the mission field than it is after you arrive.

Be sure to resolve matters now. Carrying around unconfessed and unresolved sins is like dragging your fifty-pound suitcase everywhere you go on your mission. Tracting, teaching, praying — no matter what you do — these sins will burden you wherever you are and whatever you are doing. In contrast, a clear conscience will lighten your step and give you greater confidence in all that you do. Confessing any sin is difficult for all of us. But if something is still lurking in your past then bring it to the attention of your bishop now. Through confession and sincere repentance you can leave your sins in the past and leap forward toward the spiritual and emotional rewards of your coming years of service.

While we are on the subject of repentance, all of us realize that it is much better to never take a puff of that cigarette, or listen to that dirty joke than it is to repent of having done so. In recent years, it has become a popular way of thinking for young men and women to go ahead and indulge themselves in drugs, alcohol, and other more serious sins, rationalizing that right now they will "experience" life, and later, when they reach missionary age, they will settle down, repent and go on to live a clean life as a missionary.

Don't be taken in by such shortsighted thinking. For every young person who does forsake his sinful actions, there are five who either never change or come around far too late to serve. Then they discover that they have caused themselves and others years of needless anguish. If you are tempted to sin now and pay later, consider this: repentance means remorse, that is, deep and painful regret that we have sinned. Doesn't it indicate a great lack of self-respect if you willingly do something you know you will regret later? Remember the words of President Ezra Taft Benson: "It is better to prepare and prevent than to repair and repent!" (BYU Devotional; October 14, 1987).

Occasionally missionaries enter the field who are not worthy to serve. Given the stringent demands of mission life and their own responsibility to call people to repentance, it is not long before their unresolved transgressions begin to weigh on them. There in the mission field resolving such matters is not quite as easy as it would have been before the missionary entered the field. Why wait until then? Lift the burden of sin from your shoulders now so that it doesn't hinder you then.

Great joy awaits the person who repents.

Challenge

Commit yourself to keeping all of the commandments. Start acting and dressing a little more like a missionary than you normally would. Commit yourself to not participating in filthy conversations or promiscuous activities. If you have some areas that you are concerned about, make an appointment and talk with your bishop. If appropriate, ask your own father for help in overcoming some of your problem areas. In any case, seek a priesthood blessing from your father or appropriate church authority so that you can receive additional strength to help you spiritually prepare yourself for your mission.

Just before bedtime prayers each night, evaluate what you have done with your day. Make plans for tomorrow that will move you toward your long-range goal of missionary service. Strive for a close partnership with God in making your dreams come true.

Begin now to use the power of fasting and Fast Sunday to increase your spirituality. Seek spiritual experience and be worthy of spiritual blessings.

Chapter 5

Mental Preparation

Through some strange and powerful principle
of "mental chemistry" which she has never divulged,
Nature wraps up in the impulse of strong
desire, "that something" which recognizes
no such word as "impossible", and accepts no
such reality as failure.

                        Napoleon Hill

Scriptures:
D & C 4:2, D & C 24:7, Articles of Faith 1:5

Elder Carl
California, Los Angeles Mission

I arrived in the L. A. Mission from the mission home in Salt Lake, without knowing the missionary discussions. In those days we were required to learn them in the mission field and to pass-off the discussions to our district leader and to our companions. My first companion really wanted me to learn the discussions quickly and well, so that I could teach the gospel. He didn't want me depending on my companion and trusting in him to do the teaching all the time.

As I began to memorize the discussions, we began to teach a man whose family were members of the Church. He'd gone through several sets of missionaries in the past, rejecting the gospel message each time. His home teacher, a faithful Seventy, had gone into his home and prepared him very, very well each time for the missionary discussions, although he had rejected them in past times. My companion, seeing an opportunity to help me learn the discussions, challenged me to teach this brother the discussions with the Seventy. The Seventy did not know the discussions, so it would be required of me to teach the entire discussions by myself. The first week I finished learning the first discussion and was prepared to go to this man's home and teach the discussion. Everything went very well. His desire to learn the gospel intrigued me, and gave me a tremendous desire to go and learn the other discussions. Each week as I would prepare a new discussion I felt at times as if my head would bust open. There was so much to learn, so much depended on my being able to know the discussions well enough that I could concentrate on following the spirit instead of trying to remember which word or concept came next. I really wished that I had learned them by heart before my mission.

Many times I would literally pass off a discussion minutes before going to his home to teach this man. The desire to learn the discussion and to teach the gospel message increased and filled me completely. This brother accepted the gospel with tremendous speed. His desire to learn was tremendous. I almost exploded when we completed the discussions and he accepted the gospel. But, that's not all, within a year he was in the Elders' Quorum Presidency, and right after that I had the privilege of going to the temple with him and his family to watch them be sealed for time and all eternity. Within two years of his baptism he was a member of the bishopric in his ward, and a strong, faithful member of the Church in that area.

What if I hadn't learned the discussions? What if I had just slacked off and read them to him. I am grateful that the Lord blessed me with the ability to learn my discussions well enough so that the spirit of the Lord was able to be present and that this family can now be active members in the Lord's Church.

A well-prepared missionary actually enters the field facing a tremendous mental challenge. He must know or quickly become familiar with the scriptures, the discussions, the names of investigators and members. In addition he may have to learn a new language and become familiar with local history, customs, and laws.

Repeatedly in the era of restoration, the Lord has encouraged his followers to educate their minds and hearts. And he has done this, he says,

That ye may be prepared in all things when I shall send you again to magnify the calling whereunto I have called you, and the mission with which I have commissioned you. (D & C 88:80.)

The mental challenge of a mission is indeed immense, but it is far from impossible if you prepare yourself and seek the Lord's assistance. You might even be surprised at how much you already know.

Doctrinal Basics to Learn

This is a brief overview of the doctrinal content of the missionary discussions:

1. "The Plan of our Heavenly Father": The plan of salvation; the role of Jesus Christ; the role of prophets; the mission of Joseph Smith; the Book of Mormon as a witness for Christ; the witness of the Holy Ghost.

2. "The Gospel of Jesus Christ": The resurrection; we can be saved from sin; the Atonement; faith; repentance; baptism by immersion and the proper authority; the gift of the Holy Ghost; obedience to the commandments.

3. "The Restoration": Divine truth comes from God through apostles and prophets; revelation was lost through the Apostasy; modern prophets; God has reestablished His church through Joseph Smith; We must come unto Christ through joining His church; members receive blessings through attending meetings and partaking of the sacrament.

4. "Eternal Progression": The pre-existence; the purpose of life is to learn to become like God; the spirit world; the gospel is taught in the spirit world; a family can be eternal; the law of chastity; the Word of Wisdom is a divine code of health.

5. "Living a Christlike Life": We should love God and our fellowmen; sacrifice brings blessings; fasting and fast offering bring spiritual blessings; the law of tithing.

6. "Membership in the Kingdom": Jesus Christ is our Savior, Creator, and Judge; exaltation comes through Christ; the members of the Church have a responsibility to perfect the saints, redeem the dead, and proclaim the gospel; we can follow the straight and narrow path to perfection.

It is of course essential that you as a missionary know, understand, and have a testimony of the teachings of the gospel. As mentioned before, studying and pondering the scriptures are basic parts of mental and spiritual preparation. But you can also study other works that will enhance your understanding and that you will enjoy reading. It is also important that you become familiar with the missionary discussions. (The discussions are available from the Salt Lake Distribution Center. You can order from them by calling 1-800-247-3892 outside Utah, or 1-800-782-8866 inside Utah.) You may not want to memorize them right away, but you will want to start becoming familiar with them.

For practice teaching the discussions, get together with your father, mother, brother, sister or friend and present a concept from the first discussion to him or her. You may not have memorized the discussion, but go ahead and teach it the best that you can. Have them ask you questions a non-member might ask and see what you can confidently answer. Repeat this process at regular intervals until you have taught each of the concepts of the First Discussion twice. As you begin each discussion, answer any questions you were not able to answer in the previous discussion. (You will of course in the meantime have found them out.) Repeat this until you have taught all of the discussions twice. This exercise will not only help you become familiar with the basic tenets you will be called upon to teach, but you will also learn in what order they are taught. And just as important, this exercise will also teach you what questions non-members are likely to ask you. Investigators will always ask a few questions you have never anticipated, but this exercise will prepare you for the majority of their questions. In addition, discussing and answering questions about the gospel will help you become more articulate and better able to teach the discussions in your own words.

Language Skills

One of the most frightening but enjoyable prospects of serving a mission is the chance that you may be called to a foreign country and may be required to learn a foreign language. You will want to prepare now for such a possibility by studying a foreign language of your choice. This will have several advantages. Even if you are called to an area that speaks your native tongue, learning another language teaches you important memorization and assimilation techniques. And if you are required to learn a foreign language (even if it is a different one from that which you studied) the skills you have acquired will make it easier to learn a third language or put you that much further ahead in mastering the language you have been studying.

A former Swiss Temple President is a convert to the Church who became interested because the missionaries spoke such poor German. He invited them in to satisfy his curiosity as to why they had the guts to knock on his door when they spoke the language so poorly, wondering what their message could be that was important enough to them to risk ridicule every time they opened their mouths.

Learning Ordinances and Church and Mission Procedures

Elders, you will be called on to perform some or all of the priesthood ordinances to which you hold the keys. You can quickly learn the proper procedure for consecrating oil, giving blessings of health, comfort, and counsel; for baptism and confirmation; for ordination to the priesthood; and for setting people apart for specific callings. You may also be called upon to dedicate a home or a grave. You will probably be asked to leave a blessing upon homes of members and will often bless the sick and afflicted. Depending on your age, you will quite likely be an elder for several months before your mission. Try volunteering to participate in priesthood ordinances whenever possible before you enter the mission field. You can find out how to perform these sacred ordinances by referring to the Missionary Handbook or the Melchizedek Priesthood Handbook. You should discuss them with your father and church leaders. Be sure to discuss church procedures for marriage, excommunication, probation, etc., with your bishop. Rumors about church law abound. It is better to get the facts from a reliable source.

Sisters should become familiar with the role and position that priesthood blessings take in their own lives and the lives of their converts. Understanding the nature of these ordinances can help you to better utilize their ability to bless your life and the lives of those whom you labor with.

In preparation for the mental demands of your mission follow President David O. McKay's advice and do something that's hard to do each day and smile about it.

A missionary who is alert and informed and educated **and** whose heart and mind and spirit are attuned to the Lord and His will is in an excellent position to succeed in his sacred commission.

Challenge

Try memorizing 10 of your favorite scriptures or motivational quotes or poems. Everyone of us has to learn what it takes for us to memorize something. Try to discover what *your* method is. Is it association? Timed repetitions? The only way to find out is to put your ability to memorize to the test.

Chapter 6

Social Preparation

The cure for all the ills and wrongs,
the cares, the sorrows, and the crimes
of humanity, all lie in the one word
"love." It is the divine vitality
that everywhere produces and restores life.

> Lydia Maria Child

Scriptures:
Ephesians 4:26, Psalms 89:3, John 8:1-11, John 2:15

Elder Ezra
North Carolina Mission

In one of my first areas, I heard a man who was a recent convert bear his testimony in church. As he told his conversion story, I gained an insight into an important key in missionary work. He said that before he joined the church, he always assumed that the guys riding around in pairs on bicycles and wearing white shirts and ties were members of some cultish religion that had somehow brainwashed them into leaving their homes and riding around on bikes in some far away place. When he finally had an opportunity to talk to a couple of these young men, he said, he knew for sure they were brainwashed. They tried to give him an obviously memorized speech about their beliefs and would lose their place and become frustrated whenever he asked a question. It wasn't until years later when he began a new job where one of his coworkers was a Mormon that, through several conversations with this coworker, he began to realize that the Mormons were more than a bunch of robots.

Throughout my mission, I remembered this man's story, and I strove to be a real person to the members and nonmembers I contacted. I knew that it wasn't wise to spend too much time dwelling on pre-mission life, but at the same time, I knew that conversion is a very personal thing and that my personality and experiences were important tools that I shouldn't ignore. It's been said that one of the most important factors in the conversion process is the relationship that the missionaries develop with the investigator. I know this was true in my own mission.

In one area, we attended a small gathering of members and nonmembers at a member's house. The owner of the house had a sister there who had been raised a Mormon but had long since left the Church. She had married outside the Church, and she and her husband had developed some strong anti-Mormon sentiments. As her two children were getting older, however, she began to feel a need to involve them in Church activities. We talked with her quite a bit that evening, and she said that she really felt that her husband might talk to us, even though he was so antagonistic towards the Church. When we tried to arrange an appointment to visit, though, she told us that we'd never get near her husband if we showed up wearing suits. We tried to explain to her that we had to follow the missionary dress code, but she insisted that we'd have to change into our P-day clothes if we wanted to see her husband.

This presented quite a dilemma to us, as we did not want to go against mission rules. My companion and I discussed it and decided to go ahead and visit them in our P-day clothes.

When we arrived at the farm that this family lived on, the husband was out in the yard working on a hay combine of some sort. We approached him and tried to strike up a conversation. He acknowledged our presence but kept working on the machine. My *companion had been raised on a farm in Oklahoma and offered to help fix it. Before long, they were both up to their elbows in grease, and I was passing them tools on command. We talked a lot about ourselves and where we were from, and we got to know him really well. Before we left, we arranged to come the next day to help him get up hay, on the condition that he would let us discuss the Church with him as we went along. The next day, we gave him the entire first discussion while we were walking through the hay field and also during breaks we would take, sitting next to the stream that ran through his property. Over the next few weeks, we gave him every one of the discussions in a similar manner. We taught the second discussion up on his roof, finishing off an addition to his house. Another discussion was taught while we castrated a goat that he had facetiously named Moroni. Much to his wife's surprise, he even agreed to sit down for a couple of the discussions. Finally, after about a month of this, he showed up with his family at church for the first time.*

The baptism of this man and his ten-year-old son, which took place in the stream on his land, was one of the high points of my mission. I am convinced that it never would have happened had we not made ourselves available to him on a social level and not just as missionaries. Indeed, the role of a missionary is more complex than any of us realize. We must be prepared in more than just the mechanics of discussion-giving. We are not really teaching unless someone is learning, and many people will not be able to learn from us unless they can relate to us on a personal basis.

• • •

The well-prepared missionary must have developed basic social skills. The importance of this is illustrated in the experience of Levi Edgar Young.

Before we can teach, we must get on common ground, with love and genuine understanding of the heart.

I was speaking to a man and his wife who had come to Temple Square. The man said: 'I am a Lutheran.'

had the pleasure of saying to him, 'I remember what Luther taught his people: I believe it takes the truth of the heart and soul to understand the truth of God.'

My newfound friend replied: 'I believe that.' And continuing, he asked, 'You are a great admirer of Luther?'

'Yes, very much so.'

And then as we stood there on Temple Square, the conversation turned to the restoration of the Church. When he left later, he took me by the hand, saying, 'Friend, I am now an admirer of Joseph Smith, who, you say, is a prophet of God.'

You see, we came on common ground, and he felt happy that we found something good in his belief, and I felt happier that he found something noble in mine."

The development of those social skills comes through patience, listening and a true love of Christ. In addition missionaries need to prepare so that they can express their feelings appropriately and can meet and interact well with people. Social skills also include the ability to dress and groom yourself properly and to be sensitive to and tolerant of other people's beliefs, customs, and culture.

It's easy to forget the importance of the application of these skills especially after you have been serving for a few months. A simple rule of thumb is to look in the mirror each day, and listen to what you and your companion are saying and ask yourself, "What would I think if I was a non-member who saw me or who heard what you were saying?"

Consider the words of counsel of the apostol Paul:

1 Timothy 4:12
Paul counsels Timothy in spite of his youth to be a good example in his conversations, faith, charity and purity.

1 Corinthians 13:1
Paul tells the saints that regardless of their accomplishments, if they have not charity they are as a "sounding brass, or a tinkling cymbal," or in other words, a bunch of noise.

At age 19 or 21 it is hard to imagine yourself as an ambassador. But that is exactly what you will be as a missionary — an ambassador for Christ. You are an official representative of His Church and people will judge the Church by your conduct, demeanor, and appearance.

As an ambassador you will always want to be at your best. Even though you may not feel totally at ease among strangers, and you may not be prepared for every encounter, remember that missionary work is people work. Even if you feel socially inept you can still learn to reach people. With practice you can learn to be at ease in any social situation. This confidence will come as you learn to love and respect yourself and others. And yes, you are right, now is the time to prepare.

As you come to love others, you will develop a natural sensitivity to, and respect for their practices and beliefs. For example, during your mission you will be offered alcohol, coffee, tea, and other substances that are against the Word of Wisdom. In some cultures you can offend your host by refusing offers of food or drink. But you can learn to politely decline some substances that are against your religious beliefs without offending or embarrassing your host. For example, if you are offered coffee you might say, "No, thank you, Mrs. Jones. Our religious beliefs ask us not to drink coffee, tea, or alcohol. But I would appreciate a glass of water (or whatever)." Wherever you serve, you will be confronted with a variety of social customs that differ radically from the "way we do things back home." You may not like the way local people do things. But you will offend people if you constantly tell them how superior your ways are to theirs. Therefore, for the time that you are on your mission, assume that the way they do things in your mission area is the way for you to do them, too. You must respect local customs.

Are you comfortable in social situations? If not, now is the time to prepare. Broken down into its simplest terms, your mission will mostly consist of interacting with people. You will have to daily introduce yourself to total strangers on the street, at their doorsteps, over the phone, in the market, at the homes of members, etc. Whether you are shaking hands in the local chapel, teaching a discussion in an investigator's home, or visiting a museum on preparation day, you will be under intense scrutiny. But you can become comfortable in all of these situations with just a little practice.

You can start practicing now by learning how to listen. This involves listening closely to others and giving them constant, positive feedback. You will also frequently be doing a lot of the talking. Think for a moment about the kinds of questions others might ask you that are not related directly to the missionary discussions. They will usually ask you about your home, family, goals when you return from your mission, and about why you decided to come on a mission. Think about answers you can give that have detail and that can also somehow be related to their lives and to your message. Think about how to answer someone who belittles you beliefs (I guarantee you will be in a situation where that happens. If you can answer with tact but with confidence you will usually shut the person up without embarrassing him and impress others who are listening in.)

What am I talking about?

Well, for example, let's say you drop by Mr. Caldwell's house to pick up the umbrella you accidentally left there after last night's discussion. When the Caldwells open the door, you find you have interrupted a party. Instead of handing you your umbrella, the Caldwells insist you come inside. They introduce you to their friends, who eye you curiously. You are new creatures to the Caldwells' guests, and they begin asking questions about your beliefs, some of which they find a little strange. In such a casual situation, can you comfortably answer questions about the gospel? What if they belittle your beliefs? If you can answer even barbed questions cheerfully and without embarrassment, you have a chance to influence a whole room full of people. How can you prepare? Simple—you already know part of it. Practice answering those same tough investigator questions as before but this time think of answers that will be given in a much different atmosphere than a normal teaching discussion.

You may be called to Elko, Nevada; Capetown, South Africa; Santiago, Chile; Tokyo, Japan; Sweden, Stockholm (the very best mission); or Helsinki, Finland. Wherever you are called to serve, learn to love it. After a few months in the field, you find that what matters most to you is not where you serve but how effective you are in bringing others to the gospel of Jesus Christ. The most basic tenet for loving your mission (or your job, or college, or whatever) is the ability to love yourself. You will discover that if you feel good and confident about yourself, then you will be able to feel good and confident about others. Love yourself and you will be less defensive when others attack your beliefs. Love yourself and you will succeed more because you will set goals that are realistic. Love yourself and you will have a much easier time overcoming bad habits and avoiding sin. Love yourself and you will find it easier to forgive others because you can forgive yourself. And if you love yourself now then you will understand the importance of preparation to your future happiness. And if you don't love yourself, then start right now to change. Become the best and most loyal friend you will ever have. What good will it do if you labor for the salvation of others and yet won't put forth any effort to help yourself be happy? Often missionaries are told to forget themselves, but this rarely happens if a missionary has not learned to treat himself with love and respect.

The other main factor to consider is that as you forget yourself in service to your brothers and sisters then you will find yourself. Forget your old customs, fears, prejudices and inhibitions. Immerse yourself in the culture of your mission area. Love the people, study, and pray. As you do these things you will find a happiness few possess. It comes through losing yourself.

Prepare to Serve

On my mission my goal was to become Swedish for two years. I tried to forget about America; I tried to forget about how good it was at home. I was called to serve the people of Sweden. People in other countries get offended when missionaries say things like, "Well, back in America, we do this." "We have this in America." "America's this . . . America's that. . ." What I did was say "Hey, I'm in Sweden. I'm Swedish." I wore Swedish clothes, I ate Swedish food, and I spoke Swedish. I tried as much as possible to avoid speaking English. It helped my Swedish and it helped me get closer to the Swedish people. People got really offended if we were at a bus stop or somewhere and all of a sudden we started speaking to each other in English. It's hard to be out tracting and talking about baseball games in English between doors, and then all of a sudden, switch to Swedish when someone opens the door. Quite a few of my companions and I made the rule that when we were out, we spoke nothing but Swedish. When we in our apartment, we could speak English.

I think that some people went on missions not feeling good about themselves, having sins not repented of, carrying around a lot of emotional baggage. It's like carrying around a lot of extra luggage. Missionaries who don't love themselves feel insecure about their calling. They don't feel they are worthy. They don't feel that they can do it. What eventually happens is that they end up destroying the companionship. Consequently, they do not love themselves, because of the sins they bring with them on their mission. Missionaries need to feel good about themselves. You're not going to be perfect on a mission, but realize that the Lord will accept your sacrifice and your offer, if you at least try — and try hard.

I can't stress enough the importance of loving yourself and others. Consider these words of counsel:

D & C 50:41-42
The Savior told the Church to fear not, that He had overcome the world and that no one that the Father had given Him would be lost.

Proverbs 3:5
The writer counsels us to trust in the Lord with all of our hearts and to "lean not unto our own understanding."

If you love yourself, you will be able to face the challenges of a mission with a positive attitude. Missions are full of disappointments. Many people you teach will not accept your message. The local members may let you down. Your companion and other missionaries will disappoint you. But that is part of life — that is exactly what the plan of salvation is all about. People are here choosing between right and wrong, and those who choose wrong will hurt and disappoint you. Whatever your challenges and disappointments, smile and keep moving. Keep moving, keep trying, keep enjoying your mission. Rely on your testimony, and let your light shine to all those who associate with you.

Actually, you can prepare for some of those disappointments now by finding out what they are likely to be.

It may help you to write to friends or family in the mission field or to talk with recently returned missionaries in your ward or stake. Ask them to tell you about their most common disappointments and how they learned to deal positively with them. This will add to your store of knowledge and give you more options when faced with difficulty and discouragement.

One thing that will help you keep a positive perspective is keeping a daily journal. Start now to keep your missionary journal and record your feelings about serving, about preparation, and the things about a mission that may scare you. For example, record what you think the daily routine will be like. How do you feel about having to cut your hair? What about the clothes you wear? What kind of war stories have you heard from returned missionaries? Do you believe them? What do you think you will enjoy most about your mission? What scares you the most? What kind of uplifting experiences have you had while preparing? Write down some of your preparatory goals, then record your progress from time to time. When you enter the missionary training center look back at the thoughts and experiences you have recorded. You will probably be surprised at the growth you have experienced. Continue this process throughout your mission.

Reading in your journal from time to time should bring you great strength. Reading how you overcame past disappointments and trials will help sustain you during times of discouragement. You can also use your journal as a sounding board to help you express the aspects of your mission that frustrate you. You will find that as you articulate your feelings you will be able to see the situation with greater clarity.

Here is a sample journal entry:

> *3-7-78: Elder Barber is driving me nuts. He is a good missionary but tends to get discouraged too easily. At night he usually wants to quit by 8 p.m. Last night we tried street contacting for an hour. We got the usual responses: "No thanks"; "Not interested"; "Your church is too rich"; etc. So I suggested we try going from door-to-door. Elder Barber finally agreed, but it was with great reluctance. The whole way to our tracting area he rode his bike about one mile per hour. He could tell I was steamed when we reached the neighborhood. I'm thinking of asking for a transfer.*
>
> *3-29-78: Last night Elder Barber surprised me. After our prayers he asked if we could talk. He said that he realized that he got discouraged too easily and that he knew it made me mad. Then he did something I never expected. He said, "Elder Richards, will you help me? I've given up too early throughout my life. I know I shouldn't but when the work gets hard, or boring, or cold I feel as if I can't go on any longer. I think I can change, but I can't do it alone." I asked how I could help. He said, "Pray. And encourage me when you sense it's getting tough." I felt kind of stupid, especially considering how I've made him feel when we quit early. I said I would try.*
>
> *4-29-78: I have been praying for Elder Barber for a month. At first I felt like a hypocrite, praying for him when I was sometimes annoyed with him. But after a few days I began to care more about him. I began to see how frightening trying to preach the gospel can be, especially to someone who lacks self-confidence. After two weeks I felt sincere when I hit my knees at night. But Elder Barber wasn't improving. So I began to plead with the Lord. And when we worked and I could see he was getting discouraged I would try to*

Prepare to Serve

---

cheer him up by telling him stories of Job and Elijah. After three weeks he started to show more stamina. Now he not only sticks it out, but seems to enjoy the challenge.

5-3-78: Yesterday I surprised myself. Elder Barber was transferred. As he boarded the bus, I suddenly grabbed him and embraced him. I've learned a lot praying for Elder Barber. As the bus drove off, I suddenly realized that my own trainer's long prayers into the night were not for himself; they were for me.

Developing good social skills for your mission is really just first learning to accept and love yourself (so you can forget about how *you* look and how *you* feel all the time) and then learning to focus your attention on other people instead of yourself. As you concern yourself with their uncertainties, worries, fears, and desires you will be able to act and speak with confidence and love in ways that will be comforting and helpful to them.

Challenge

From this day on practice social skills with your own family and friends. Think about what you are going to say before you say it. Be tactful, be patient, smile more, listen more and talk less. Spend a few extra minutes a day grooming yourself. Try looking people directly in the eye when they talk with you. Focus your attention on "one" of their eyes, and smile. When you walk, hold your head erect and straight. Remember who you represent.

Develop the kind of personality you like to be around. A friendly smile, a firm handshake, and a happy manner are always appreciated. Politeness in all things is the mark of a true LDS missionary. Politeness has nothing to do with a person's age. It has to do with one's capacity for successfully relating to other people. Doing these things will make a difference. Use them every day for the rest of your mission and life.

Chapter 7

Financial Preparation

What this power is I cannot say; all
I know is that it exists and it becomes
available only when a man is in that
state of mind in which he knows exactly
what he wants and is fully determined
not to quit until he finds it.

> Alexander Graham Bell

Scriptures:
Luke 14:28; D & C 75:23,26; 3 Nephi 24:8-10

Elder Henry
Florida, Tallahassee Mission

I was introduced to the church by a guy in my typing class my sophomore year in high school. We sat next to each other because we knew each other from third grade. He asked me if I'd like to come out and play basketball with his church team.

"What church is that?"

"The Mormon church; the Church of Jesus Christ of Latter-Day Saints."

I had never heard the word Mormon, let alone Latter-Day Saints. I was raised a Catholic; my brother was a Catholic; my

Prepare to Serve

girlfriend was Presbyterian; and my sister and father were both Seventh-Day Adventists. I was fairly well exposed to different religions, but obviously not enough to know about the Mormons. I went and participated in their sports and started going to their church a little bit. Probably the biggest key to my attendance was that I just felt "right" there. I had a good feeling when I went into the chapel. Something about it made me know I should go there.

After I graduated from high school, the missionaries taught me. For a long time I didn't even realize that I had a testimony. I thought I had to read the entire Book of Mormon and get the burning in my bosom before I could say for sure that the Church was true. I was approaching it very methodically, but I thought that was the way I was supposed to.

I went to Oregon State, still unbaptized, and was in a fraternity there. I didn't drink; I knew it was wrong because of the teachings of the Gospel. In my fraternity the guys would say, "Are you a Mormon?" And I'd say, "Oh, no, no. I'm not LDS." But then if anyone would ask me about the Church, I'd just get out one of the copies of the Book of Mormon I brought with me and try to get them to read it.

Back home that summer everything bad happened to me financially. I backed up into a little car with my four-wheel-drive uninsured pick-up truck. Then my "guaranteed" job that I'd had for two summers was not available because the owner had a friend who had a lawyer who had a son who needed a job more, even though I had set all kinds of records in canning paint at this paint factory. Next, my truck was stolen. I didn't have theft insurance either. All my life savings went down the tube. Everything fell apart — no job, the accident to pay for, and the biggest asset that I had at the time was stolen.

My friend, Kelly Homer, the one who first got me to play basketball, had been on a mission for about six months. I was talking and joking with his father one day. I said, "Gosh, I know that when I join the church all this stuff will be taken care of." I kept attempting to read the Book of Mormon. Each time I'd start from the beginning because I *felt that I had to read it from start to finish. Then I asked if I could just pick up where I had left off. Kelly's father said, "Well, certainly. You can pick up where ever you want." I still had in my mind that I had to finish the Book of Mormon, so I kept attempting. I finally got so fed up that I decided I'd read the Book of Mormon in one sitting. I started one morning, and finished that night.*

Then I sat down to pray hoping that I'd feel that burning in the bosom. Nothing was coming. Then a question popped into my mind, which I later found out was one of the committing questions we ask our investigators. It was: Ask yourself if this book is true. So, I asked myself. Then I thought, "Well, of course, I know this book is true. It's history. I honestly believe that what I just read was history." Then, I thought, "Well, wait a minute. What does that mean?" Then I proceeded to commit myself. I said, "If the Book of Mormon is true, that means Joseph Smith had to have been a true prophet." The Lord would not bring forth a false book through a true prophet or vice versa. He would have to use someone who was a true man of God, so if he's a true prophet then I guess that the church has to be true, along with all the principles it stands for. I felt great! I proceeded to go upstairs and call Kelly who was on his mission in Canada. I told him that I knew the Church was true, and I was joining it. Of course, he was very excited.

That night I received a phone call from a friend in my fraternity that I hadn't talked to since the Spring Semester had let out. I got a job with his father in the construction industry. The first week I made $800.00.

Next I got my truck back. So, the Lord works in mysterious ways. I got the job. I made money. After I joined the Church, I found out that I had to wait a year before I could go on my mission, which I wasn't too happy about. I started saving all the money that I could for my mission. The time was drawing near for my mission, and I was short of the financial goal I had set. I had tried to sell my truck for at least an average value. It was very hard at that time, because that was during that gas crisis, and people weren't that excited about buying a full-sized truck. I had about four or five thousand dollars, but I was about two thousand dollars short. It was the day before I was supposed to leave, and I did not know what to do. I just kept praying to somehow find the extra money.

Out of the blue the father of a young lady that I used to see socially said that he would lease the truck from me for approximately one hundred dollars a month. He needed a truck for hauling wood and trash and all his needs at home. He had a large family. So, that was the other 2,000-2,400 dollars that I needed.

When I came home from my mission, I was basically penniless. It was right down to the wire. I had kept a strict budget. I know to this day where every penny went. The mission average financially was about 200-250 dollars a month, and I was spending as low as 140 dollars a month. I really watched my money closely. Since I have joined the church, I've not had a blind faith towards finances, but I've always felt that if I work hard, and do what is right, and have a lot of "works" as well as faith, the Lord will take care of me. He always has taken care of me. I've never really had to beg for a job. They have always been there, and they've always paid well. Since my mission, I've always been fairly well off financially.

• • •

As a missionary, you have a stewardship not only over a part of the Lord's vineyard but also over some of His money. Regardless of where the money for your mission comes from, once it has been earmarked as missionary funds, it is sacred. It doesn't matter if you have a money orchard back home, while you're a missionary you must spend frugally and wisely.

In the *Missionary Handbook*, there is a section on "Finances" found on pages 30-33. First, it says to "Budget your money carefully, and keep expenses to a minimum." All missionaries should be on a budget and should keep a record of the money they spend each month. Missionaries are also instructed to stay out of debt, including with companions. Missionaries

Prepare to Serve

---

must pay all bills before leaving an area, so you should keep a small reserve in a checking account for transfers and other unexpected expenses. Missionaries are also advised to "Avoid wasting money on souvenirs and other unnecessary items."

The estimated expenses for a mission are included in a call letter from the Missionary Department and are included in a semi-annual report sent to bishops. As you consider your own financial preparation, take time to discuss with your bishop what your average monthly expenses will be. He can give you realistic figures. There are numerous challenges in the mission field, and worrying about how to pay the rent or purchase a pint of milk should not be among them. As you ponder the overall budget for your mission, ask several recently-returned missionaries how they spent their money and how they might have spent it differently.

Some missionaries spend as much or more money on cameras, film, film development, souvenirs, etc., as they do on food. Learn to manage your funds wisely. Following is a list of expenses you will encounter before and on your mission:

Pre-Mission Expenses

- Physical and dental examinations (and any necessary treatment)

- Passport or travel document (whether you think you will go on a foreign mission or not)

- Required mission photographs of yourself

- Missionary clothes (suits, ties, shirts, undergarments, shoes, over coats, white clothes for baptism)

- Personal items (razors, soap, toothpaste, toothbrushes, writing paper, a journal)

- Travel expenses to the Missionary Training Center (MTC) and to your mission
- Cost of staying at the MTC
- A set of scriptures in your native tongue

Mission Expenses

- Travel to district and zone conferences
- Initial bicycle, mass transit pass or car expenses
- Bicycle / Automobile repairs
- Travel expenses for transfers
- Gifts for your family and friends / Souvenirs for yourself

Monthly Mission Expenses

- Monthly food and rent
- Monthly car rental / gas
- Monthly mass transportation card
- Food
- Postage
- Laundry and dry cleaning
- Fast Offerings

- Telephone, electricity and other utility expenses for your apartment

- Recreational Expenses on Preparation day.

You may also have to pay for:

- Scriptures and a dictionary in a foreign language

- A visa or residency permit

- Vaccinations

- A few select books (such as *Jesus the Christ*) as required by your mission president

- Bathing Facilities

- A sleeping bag

- Any medical treatment you receive as a missionary

It is important that you earn at least a portion of your mission funds. You will discover that sacrifices made before your mission will give added meaning to your time of service. In addition, missionaries who earn their own money for their missions tend to be especially careful with their funds.

Parents and families of prospective missionaries should be thinking and planning and saving in advance. The Church expects that every missionary family will supply at least part of the support for its missionary. This is vitally important for the family, for the missionary, and for the work.

Missionary work is a labor of love and unselfishness and derives no small part of its efficacy from the sacrifice and devotion of the people who help to support missionaries. It would be good if every missionary were able to support himself at least in part by funds he had earned himself and had saved for that special purpose.

Some things that may help you in preparing financially for your mission include buying some clothes which you could wear both before and during your mission (and after if they last that long). With some careful shopping you can find clothes that you will want to wear both on and off your mission. And if you find clothes you feel good in, you will have greater confidence in those never-ending social situations we discussed earlier. You might also ask that Christmas and birthday presents be mission-oriented.

Regardless of the source of your financial support, use the funds you receive wisely. They are sacred funds that you or others have consecrated to the Lord to sustain you temporally while you preach the gospel. Be cautious when considering purchases for your mission. Expensive cameras or recording equipment can prove a distraction to you and an added expense that your budget really cannot afford. For this very reason many mission presidents request that missionaries not bring expensive cameras with them into the field. I am not suggesting that you should feel guilty for snapping a few photos or buying some souvenirs, but use your money prudently and you will enjoy your mission more.

You should consider getting a small notebook, copying the form on the next page and begin today tracking your expenses. As has already been mentioned, your missionary funds are sacred. By tracking your expenses you not only will be aware of what you are spending, but you will also develop a pattern of success for your life after your mission and have an excellent record of your mission.

Prepare to Serve

Missionary Budgeting Sheet

Date	Expense Description	Amount	Necessary?	Deposit	Source Amount	Balance

Prepare to Serve

Missionaries who mismanage their funds can also cause problems in their companionship. A missionary who spends more than he should on preparation day outings or expensive snacks or meals likewise forces his companion to shoulder added financial burdens. A missionary who overspends is also likely to want to borrow money from his companion which places his companion in an awkward position. He may want to help his companion as his friend, but, being forbidden by mission rules and perhaps by his own financial circumstances, he cannot help his spendthrift companion. No matter what, he will be embarrassed.

Just as a conditioned, healthy athlete is a greater asset to a basketball team than one who is out of shape, so a prepared missionary can make a greater contribution to the Lord's work than one who is not prepared. Talent and genius can never take the place of preparation. There are many in the world who are always seeking for the secret to success. You probably know a few yourself. But those who are successful know that there are no secrets to success. The principles of success are well-known. The difference is that those who are successful apply the principles that work. Of course, that is an oversimplification. Every prospective missionary will have had various degrees of financial, educational, spiritual, social, and family opportunities. You will find that you are more prepared in some aspects and less prepared in others than are each of your companions. But regardless of the opportunities you have had up until now, you can still acquire the traits you need to be happy and to succeed. Success comes by applying true principles, not seeking for quick and easy roads to happiness.

You can learn a language, overcome shyness, keep within a budget or do anything else with the Lord's help. You can effect these changes by prayerfully evaluating your strengths and weaknesses. As you do so, be honest about your personal characteristics; ask your Heavenly Father to help you turn your weaknesses into strengths. Then follow the promptings of the Spirit and they will guide you towards needed changes and help.

Prepare to Serve

President Ezra Taft Benson gave the following words of advice during the April 6, 1985 General Priesthood Session:

Yes, young men, prepare now [for your missions]. Prepare yourselves physically, mentally, socially, and spiritually.

Always be obedient to authority. Start a savings account for your mission if you haven't done so already. Pay your tithing, and seek a testimony of the gospel through study and prayer.

Getting your finances in order prior to entering the MTC will free you from unnecessary stress while you are studying and while you serve your mission. Take the responsibility for making financial plans yourself — how to get the money together and how to apply the funds once you are in the mission field — doing so will give you an extra measure of control over your mission experience and an extra measure of satisfaction from knowing that you served your mission being able to concentrate on the message and the people to be reached, and not worrying constantly about finances.

Challenge

If you haven't already started a missionary savings plan, now is the time to do it. Anticipate, by using the expense categories that were mentioned in this Chapter, how much money you will need for you mission. Then divide up how much time you have left until you serve and estimate how much you will have to save or earn. If the figure is staggering, don't be overwhelmed. If it looks like you are going to come up a little bit short, you could consider selling something like your penny collection or consider working an extra job.

Apply the principles of prayer and faith. My scout group several years ago "adopted" a South American Elder to send a care package to. This Elder had left on his mission having sold every worldly possession he had. His home branch had bought him a suit and a white shirt. His faith impressed each of my scouts. As we had fund raiser after fund raiser our excitement increased as we were able to send the biggest, heaviest missionary care package that has ever been sent. Each of my boys was blessed with the missionary spirit as we sent this missionary not only some necessary items, but also our love for him and his dedication to service.

Develop the kind of faith which this South American Elder had, and be willing to accept the help of others after you have done everything that you can do yourself.

Chapter 8

Practical Preparation

History has demonstrated that the
most notable winners usually encountered
heartbreaking obstacles before they
triumphed. They won because they refused to
become discouraged by their defeats.

B.C. Forbes

Scriptures:
D & C 88:119, D & C 88:90, D & C 88:80

Elder Brent
Korea, Seoul Mission

Well, I figured I was as prepared as anyone when I left for my mission. I mean, I was no spiritual giant, but I had finished three and a half years of seminary and even managed to stay awake through part of it. Financially, I had done as much as could be expected of a nineteen-year-old kid. I started my missionary savings account when I was a Deacon (with a certain amount of "encouragement" from the parents). Of course, there were a lot of unexpected financial demands during my high school years, like that old Camaro my dad didn't want me to get and the trip to California with the guys that one summer. I must admit that there was a lot less in the account than I thought there would be when it was time to go, but what the heck, my father could use the blessings.

Prepare to Serve

I hadn't been in the MTC very long, though, when I began to realize that there might have been one area of preparation that I had overlooked. This revelation came to me while walking to the bus-stop by the MTC one P-day. I was clowning around with one of the other elders, and, in the middle of my "Kung-fu" imitation, the seat of my pants ripped wide open. Now, they have a nurse at the MTC, a cafeteria, a post office, a gym, and I hear that they even have a barber shop now. The one thing I couldn't find, however, was a pants-sewer-upper. This was, I concluded, a gross oversight in planning, but it still left me with my garments in the wind and not a mother in sight. Well, you know what they say about necessity and invention. I was forced to improvise. The staples lasted for a couple of months, but I never did get the rust spots out. I had less success with my idea to use Elmer's glue to put a button back on my shirt. The sucker popped right off. Who cared, anyway. For all I knew, they didn't even have buttons in Korea.

Once I got to Korea, I was in for more than a few rude awakenings. The people are the most beautiful people in the world, but nobody ever told me that they eat rotten cabbage. And there I was; the only thing I could cook was Fruit Loops, and I couldn't even locate the necessary ingredients for that. In the middle of my dilemma, fate or guardian angels or something entered: Elder J became my new companion.

Elder J came from a very large but very close family somewhere in Idaho, and his mother had taught him how to do a lot of things that most guys don't know how to do. What's more surprising is that he evidently was paying attention. Elder J could cook, clean, shop and sew better than any other elder (or sister, for that matter) that I've ever known. He even made the drapes for the mission home. Once, while we were companions, he gave a Relief Society lesson on the finer points of canning.

In addition to saving my life, Elder J's many talents also proved useful in finding investigators. We were given the opportunity of setting up a booth at a local festival, but it was with the stipulation that we not *actively proselyte. Elder J came up with the idea that we set up a quilting booth. Amidst the scoffs and laughs of the rest of the zone, he explained the details of his plan. The quilt would not be an ordinary quilt. On each of the center patches of the quilt would be a principle of the restored Gospel: priesthood authority, continuing revelation, genealogy, family home evening, etc. The booth would be set up as a demonstration of quilting techniques, but, hopefully, the patches on our display and the strange, clean-cut young Americans surrounding it would generate curiosity about the Church.*

Before long, every elder in the zone was working on the largest missionary tract ever devised. Busily quilting away, I couldn't help thinking, "If my mother could see me now." Not only was our quilting expertise a big hit at the festival, but we also got a large number of referrals. We were able to teach several choice individuals as a result of Elder J's clever idea.

Looking back on my experiences with Elder J, I can't say that knowing how to quilt should be a prerequisite for missionary service, but I can see how any missionary would be a lot better off if he knew how to do a few basic things that he usually depends on his mother to do.

• • •

Thus far we have discussed spiritual, mental, and financial preparation. By now you have hopefully discussed these aspects of your mission with parents and bishop and any others who might help you. But there are some other factors of practical preparation. These are not as difficult to deal with, but are worthy of mention since they will affect your overall well-being. It is important that you know how to maintain your body as well as your mind and spirit. Maintain is a good word because with proper care your body will be able carry you through those cold winter days and hot summer afternoons, up endless rows of steps, and along thousands of miles of road.

Knowing how to cook more than toast and oatmeal and how to keep yourself, your apartment and your clothes clean and in good repair will save you much time and money. But this maintenance will have an added psychological benefit. A healthy body that is dressed in clean, neat clothes (and sleeps, eats and studies in a clean apartment) will help you feel more confident, energetic and organized.

Cleanliness *is* next to Godliness. The Spirit of God will not dwell in an unclean place — and that goes for your room as well as your body!

Physical Preparedness

"And the spirit and the body are the soul of man."(D&C 88:15.) The spirit *and* the body. We usually think of missionary work as being very spiritual in nature, but I guarantee that your spirit is not going anywhere that your body doesn't feel like taking it. Taking care of your body is a responsibility that the Lord expects you to take seriously. With a little foresight, there are several things that you can do in preparation to ensure that your flesh will be as willing as your spirit throughout your mission.

Few things contribute more to your overall well-being than a well-balanced diet, physical exercise and the proper amount of sleep. Not many missionaries have trouble sleeping. Indeed, you will find that you will sleep better on your mission than any other time in your life. However, some missionaries stay up too late studying or oversleep in the mornings with the guaranteed result that their physical and mental conditions will suffer. As a missionary, you will be expected to be up by 6:30 each morning and in bed by 10:30 each night (*Missionary Handbook* p.11). Set a goal to start living by the missionary schedule now, instead of waiting until you get to the MTC. That'll be one less adjustment you'll have to make and it will bring your life more into line with gospel teachings and the counsel of the prophets. Read D & C 88:124.

In D&C 88 the Lord counseled his people to be active and take control of their own lives by avoiding idleness in action and speech and by practicing good sleeping habits which would give their bodies energy and vigor. This counsel applies doubly to missionaries.

Prepare to Serve

Missionary work is extremely demanding and imposes heavy physical and emotional strains. One who is preparing for a mission call should be thinking of this demand. A missionary who is not well cannot do the work, and his companion and others and the work itself all suffer serious interference.

In the MTC you will learn a regimen of calisthenics and other exercises that you will practice throughout your mission. Now, of course, riding your bike 60 kilometers a day and walking up thousands of steps will help keep you fit. But if you will follow the missionary handbook and exercise every day, you will find you have much more energy and will be less prone to depression. You can prepare for the physical demands of a mission by involving yourself in a regular exercise program now. Even if it's just a few simple calisthenics in the morning or a brisk daily walk through the neighborhood, you'll be surprised how much better you'll feel if it's done on a consistent basis. Now would also be a good time to take those extra couple of pounds off. No sense taking any excess baggage on your mission.

As we talked about in the beginning of this book, compiling some recipes before your mission can contribute much to your happiness while there. You need to keep a few things in mind when compiling mission recipes:

One, they must be simple. You won't have two hours to spend in the kitchen each day. Dishes that can be prepared in twenty minutes or less are desirable. They should also consist of ingredients that can be found in almost any country. You may also be doing all of your cooking on a hot plate and have limited refrigeration.

Two, they must be nutritious. Look for recipes that utilize vegetables. Be sure to add fresh fruits and vegetables to all of your meals.

Three, they must be inexpensive. Food cooked at home is inexpensive, unless it is too extravagant.

Four, you should "test drive" each recipe before you ever leave home. Get your mother to help you compile recipes and then offer to cook them each Sunday night. If your family survives, then the recipes and your cooking will be fine for you and your companion.

There are some other things you can do to be better prepared for your mission in a practical sense. Get your mother or someone else to teach you how to sew on a button or mend a ripped seam. Offer to clean the bathroom some Saturday morning with them supervising and giving helpful tips. You probably won't have to do too much arm-twisting on that one. Have them show you how to defrost a refrigerator. These are things you need to know. Above all, make sure to have fun preparing for your mission. These precious memories with your family and loved ones will be yours forever.

Be sure to resolve all medical and dental problems before entering the MTC. Problems or potential problems such as wisdom teeth, ingrown toenails, damaged joints, poor vision, etc, should be taken care of before you ever leave for your mission. Not only can they hamper your ability to serve, but they can also be very expensive. There is also the risk that you may be in an area where you cannot receive adequate medical care. I know these things don't sound like any big deal right now. But how are you going to radiate the joy of the gospel when your wisdom teeth have made your gums tender and swollen? Try tracting all day with an ingrown toenail. Try memorizing the discussions in Finnish when the words just kind of blur together. Suddenly those "little things" won't seem so little. Why let that happen to a nice person like you? Take care of those "little things" now.

In accepting ourselves and in accepting, appreciating, and serving our Father's other children, we are showing our love for him. This is one of the most important ways to be preparing to serve the Lord. Make and follow good health habits (including cooking nutritious meals), learn to maintain your own clothing and dwelling, and learn, by practice, to love and serve your fellow man.

Prepare to Serve

Challenge

Read "Health" in the *Missionary Handbook*, pp. 28-29. Start preparing at least one meal a week for your family (that includes cleaning up after yourself and washing the dishes). Begin to follow a regular program of exercise. Start living by the missionary schedule: arise by 6:30 and retire by 10:30.

You are what you eat. Balanced meals develop a balanced body and mind. Learn what a balanced meals is and start eating right.

Determine to sew on your own buttons and sew your own seams starting now while Mom is there to teach you how.

Chapter 9

Social Ties in Missionary Preparation

Love is everything. It is the key to
life, and its influences are those that
move the world.

> Ralph Waldo Trine

Scriptures:
Enos 1-10, 1 Corinthians Chapter 13, Romans 13:8

Sister Julie
South Africa, Capetown Mission

    Before my mission, I knew I had a testimony, but I didn't know what to do with it, or how strong it was. I guess that I lacked confidence in my testimony. But to be quite honest, I really felt the same way about a lot of things. I hadn't yet learned the lesson that with a testimony, or with the Spirit, comes the responsibility of developing it and using it for the building of the Kingdom of the Lord. Through my experiences before my mission I have come to realize that the Lord does intervene and help us achieve our potential and develop our talents. He loves us very much and want us to be fully prepared for the challenges that may face us in the future. I learned this in a very specific and yet extremely personal way.

Prepare to Serve

When I first got to BYU, I didn't have very much social confidence. I don't think I'd ever really seen the gospel at work touching and changing peoples lives. I had especially never seen it work through me. At BYU, I got into a ward that was very active. It was really neat; the entire ward was filled with the spirit that comes from working together. Everyone really seemed to care for each other. There were some very strong people in the ward. My first job in the ward was to put together the newsletter. But to be quite honest, I didn't do a very good job. I regret that to this day. I never really learned through that calling how the Gospel can touch others' lives, or how it works in others' lives.

Then, in August of 1984, they reorganized the Relief Society Presidency. I remember when I was told I had an appointment with the Bishop, the thought came into my mind, "They haven't called a Secretary yet. Uh-ah, no-way, not me." I always had the idea that the ladies in the Relief Society Presidency were kind of different from everyone else. Anyway, I went to see the Bishop and sure enough I was called to be the Secretary in the Relief Society Presidency. I wasn't quite sure of what all that would entail, but I knew one thing was that I would have to become more spiritual.

It was a lot more responsibility than I had even dreamed. I now had to work directly with people —I mean very directly. I was kind of in shock after they called me. I couldn't believe it was me. I guess another thing that I couldn't really understand yet was the fact that I could be used as an instrument of Heavenly Father. The scriptures and my church leaders have always talked about listening to and following the spirit. I was always used to having someone other than the Lord tell me what to do. Maybe this calling would help me develop that spiritual quality.

Well, that very evening that I accepted my new call, even before I was set apart, we had our first presidency meeting. We needed to put together the Visiting Teaching program for the ward (match up the companionships and assign them sisters to visit teach.) As we got started, I *began to realize that this was a big job, and began to feel concerned that we only had a three hour meeting to get all of it accomplished. I remember sitting there, trying to decide which girl should go with which girl. As we began to realize the importance of these companionships and assignments, we began to be humbled by the importance and weight of our decisions. As we began to realize our own weaknesses, we as a group called upon the Lord for help. For the first time in my life I saw the Spirit of the Lord put companionships together; our Heavenly Father who had so much of what I thought was so important to worry about like Nuclear War, etc., that night visited our meeting with his spirit to help us put something so simple as the Visiting Teaching program together. I gained a testimony of Visiting Teaching because I saw the Lord directing it. I knew He wouldn't direct it if it wasn't for our good.*

The thing that amazed me is that while we were working I would say, "Well, what about this person, or that person?" Then someone else would say, "You know I was thinking the same thing." Then another person would say, "No, I don't feel right about it," or the President would say, "I don't feel good about that." At times we would be talking about a person and trying so hard to put one girl with a companionship. We didn't know who to put her with. Who would be able to touch her the most? All of the sudden we would say a certain companionship, and all of us would stop and say, "Yes! That is the one." I remember feeling this calm, happy feeling. I had never felt that before. I didn't know it really worked like that. I had heard about it, but didn't know it could work that way with me. It touched me so much. The thing that meant so much was to know that the Lord would actually have His Spirit work through me to touch someone else's life in a very positive way.

Throughout my time in the Presidency, I can remember so many happy moments in Presidency Meetings. We'd be discussing the welfare of the girls and the Spirit would come as we'd be speaking about the Gospel. Then we'd take that Spirit with us to our other meetings, and it would touch the other girls. In addition to learning about the use of the spirit, my calling also helped teach me the importance of preparation.

Prepare to Serve

We had a habit, as a Presidency, of going into Relief Society and sitting down and scanning all the girls during opening exercises. We could pick out the girls that needed an extra special "hello", or someone who needed a hug. Most of the time we were right. I remember one particular time, I noticed this one girl looked particularly sad. I watched her, then afterward I went up and gave her a hug. It helped her. I remember how good it felt to actually be able to help someone. I think what it taught me was to stop, use the stewardship and leadership that was upon me, and let the Spirit work through me. I had never seen it like that before.

By accepting this call to serve in the Relief Society, I had accepted far more than I realized then. I had also accepted the call to help prepare me for my mission. A lot of Elders and Sisters avoid Church calls before their missions thinking, "Well, I'll be working full-time then, so right now, I am going to have fun." At BYU I could have done a million things instead of spending the time that I did serving in my student ward's relief society presidency. But nothing would have prepared me with the social, leadership and spiritual qualities that I needed so desperately to serve as a good missionary as that did.

Just as I was putting in my mission papers, I was up on the Temple grounds on a Sunday afternoon thinking and praying about some things which were on my mind. It was a beautiful day. I felt really good about myself and about my decision to serve as a full time missionary. As I was leaving that day I noticed a lady getting out of a car. I also saw that she was by herself with a car full of children. Feeling prompted to do so, I went down and offered to help her take the kids out. As we lifted them out, for some reason she just began talking to me. She told me she had an inactive husband. She said that she couldn't understand it. He was a returned missionary; they had been married in the Temple; but still he was inactive. As she spoke, the Spirit bore witness to me about how troubled she was. I knew at that moment she felt like she wasn't worth anything. In fact, I sensed that she felt like she had failed. I also knew that she still felt like she really was supposed to have married her husband.

Prepare to Serve

As I stepped back and looked, I saw a woman who was confused and unhappy, but mostly her self-esteem was hurting. As I spoke with her, she began to cry. Following the Spirit's counsel, I told her that I felt like the Lord needed her to know that "Yes, she was doing okay, and she was doing a good job." That is all she needed to know. The Lord was saying to her, "Hey, you're doing right." When she heard this, she cried, and we hugged. We talked for quite a while more, and I literally saw her spirit lift, but it wasn't me who was doing it. It was the girl who a while before didn't know that the Lord could work through her.

Right then, with the Lord using me as an instrument at that moment, my testimony grew about three sizes. I felt like I was going to burst. This lady who was so burdened down in despair needed the Lord. She needed her Heavenly Father, but she needed a direct touch. So that day he used one of His other children to talk with her. That way she could have a direct communication; something tangible sitting by her, some love. I knew that the Lord was helping me help this girl, and as I drove away I was on cloud nine. I thought, "Yes, the Lord can use me as His instrument." I had never known that before, but it was taught to me because I was given the stewardship of helping those girls. That taught me that when you have a testimony you can also gain the social confidence and the self confidence to know that the Spirit can work through you. But the only way you are taught that is by actually experiencing it. That is what the social interaction in that Presidency helped me to understand — that it was possible for me to be used as an instrument. It helped me to become more aware of others' feelings and to become more responsible for the welfare of others.

As I went into the mission field, I carried that responsibility and stewardship with me, intending to give my all to serve the Lord, and to serve His children in South Africa.

• • •

Prepare to Serve

So... you have six months to go before you can submit your papers. Take a moment to consider this period in your life. You will realize that this is a great opportunity to form lasting friendships with the many people who help you prepare for your mission. While the primary purpose of a mission is to bring the gospel to non-members, your years of full-time service to the Lord will affect many of your relatives and friends.

As you talk with friends, parents, returned missionaries and co-workers about your upcoming mission you will cause them to reflect upon the meaning of God in their lives. Those who are members of the Church will reflect with gratitude on the blessings of the gospel and will often reminisce about their own times of service. Those who are not members of the Church or who are less-active members will feel a greater desire to know more about God and the meaning of life. Take a moment right now and count how many people your mission will affect. Record those with whom you would like to remain in contact. Then when you reach the mission field, write them a letter from time to time and share your experiences and testimonies with them. Many non-member friends and associates will have an intense interest in your welfare and will be greatly flattered that you would think enough of them to stay in touch.

If you think back on your life, there are many people who have influenced you: Seminary teachers, school teachers, Bishops, etc. It's easy to get wrapped up in missionary work, and we sometimes forget the influence of a quick note. A short note to your Bishop, Seminary teacher or other people in your home ward is always greatly appreciated — just a quick note telling them how your mission is going and thanking them for their support. This not only makes them feel that you care, but it also blesses them for the efforts they made in helping you get there. It also serves as a testimony builder when you relate a neat experience you have had. Just let yourself communicate. Give a little extra time. It doesn't cost that much. In most foreign countries you can get letter grams.

I have two friends — Lee and Brian. We were all called on missions at the same time. We wanted to keep in contact, but the letters just seemed to get a little silly. So what we started doing was: I sent a tape that was a

Prepare to Serve

---

c-60. I talked on a half-hour of it, then sent it to Lee, who was in South Africa. Lee listened to my half-hour, then he taped on the other side for a half-hour, and sent it to Brian, who was in South America. Brian listened to both my side of the tape and to Lee's side, and then erased over my side, while he taped a half-hour. So we just kept this going back and forth for two years. Each of us would be able to hear the other two half-hours of the tape. When it came back to me there would be Lee and Brian on the tape. When it went to Lee, there would be Brian and myself. When it went to Brian, there would be Lee and myself. It just kept going that way. It was fun to keep close contact with these friends. I used to get a little jealous about how they were baptizing hoards of converts in South America. Seems like all they did was just go and baptize everyone. Lee had a tough mission is South Africa. It was fun to hear from them both, and get words of encouragement.

There was a young man who had grown up in my ward, and at about the age of sixteen he started really going off the deep end. More than just going off the deep end, he was down there. He was down as deep as you can go. David ended up running away from home, working on a banana boat headed for South Africa. David really experienced the bad part of the world. Finally, David came home and it was kind of like the prodigal son. He was a handsome and talented young man, from one of the strongest families in the ward, and he'd really gone off the track. But when he came home the ward welcomed him. The Bishop, as part of his counselling and to help him prepare for his mission, assigned David the choice task of being a pre-missionary. David was assigned to work with the Stake missionaries and help fellowship some part-member families in the ward. I'll never forget how David took an inactive family that was having quite a bit of trouble and financial difficulties under his wing. David became the big brother in that house. He became the person who helped them fix their house. During that next year David experienced true love. That is one of the reasons he went on a mission. He forgot himself for awhile, and some of the things he'd been doing, and started really giving of himself to someone else. As a young person I watched this and was very impressed with the sincerity he had. I know that family to this day. Even though they do not see David as much anymore, they will never forget the help he gave them.

Because of this young man's efforts, that family became active, they got on their feet, and the children started doing what they should. David truly became a disciple of Christ.

Being a missionary isn't something mystical that only perfect people can manage; it is following Christ's admonition to love your fellow men and do unto them as you would have them do unto you. It isn't looking for perfect people to bring into the Church; it is helping people to improve themselves and their circumstances so they will be able to accept the Spirit of Truth into their lives.

Challenge

No matter how young or old you are start now to involve your family and friends in your missionary preparation. Talk with them about your desires to serve and make them a very real part of your mission experience.

Seek out counsel from parents, friends, brother and sisters, teachers, leaders and your Bishop.

Begin to do acts of love and kindness for those around you who are in need of friendship and strengthening.

Chapter 10

Preparation at the Missionary Training Center

Most successful men have not
achieved their distinction by having
some new talent or opportunity presented
to them. They have developed the
opportunity that was at hand.

>   Bruce Barton

Scriptures:
D & C 58:14, D & C 130:20,21

Elder Thomas
Hawaii, Mission

I think I was quite possibly the least prepared missionary to ever enter the MTC. I had been baptized a year before by two persistent missionaries down in the deep South, and until I met them, I had never seen a Mormon in my entire life. In fact, I had never even heard of the Mormon church. I think I remember once seeing an advertisement somewhere for The Church of Jesus Christ of Latter-day Saints, and I just assumed it was some Catholic-related church since it believed in Saints.

Very soon after my baptism I started feeling strongly that I should go on a mission. I thought it was more than coincidence that the

Prepare to Serve

Good Lord sent the missionaries to my life ten months before my nineteenth birthday. When I submitted my papers, there was still so much about the Church I didn't know, though. When I got my mission call, for example, I couldn't figure out for the life of me why I had to go to some place called Provo, Utah, first when my mission was supposed to be in Hawaii. The Missionary Training Center was something that had not been mentioned to me before.

When it was time to go, I decided to drive across the country instead of fly, even though the Church would pay for the plane ticket. A member of the ward needed a car driven out to his kids at BYU, and I was excited about the adventure.

I arrived at the MTC on the appointed day and walked in a little late to my orientation meeting. I had brought a couple of suits and some white shirts, but nobody had told me I was supposed to dress up for the MTC. I walked in the room with my jeans on and sporting a mustache that I hadn't shaved off in three years. Having disrupted the meeting, I was feeling pretty awkward. The other missionaries were all spiffed up in their new clothes and had brought along their entire families to bid them farewell. An older gentleman came over to ask me what I wanted, and I told him that I was going to be a missionary. He left me and walked back across the room and consulted with another man who was looking at some papers in his hand. He looked up, and I heard him say, "Yes. His name's on the list." The first man walked back over to me and told me to have a seat and to come talk to him after the meeting. When the meeting was over, I was taken to BYU in a van with some other missionaries to get my hair cut.

Things didn't get any better the second day. We sat in class all day long, and I felt like a one-legged man in a can-kicking contest. I didn't know if Alma was in the New Testament or the Old Testament. For all I knew, it could have been in the Doctrine and Covenants.

On the third day I didn't go to the morning class. I stayed in my room and had the longest prayer of my entire life. I had heard about

Prepare to Serve

Enos praying all day and all night, and I decided that I wouldn't stop praying until I knew whether I should stick it out or just quit and go home. I didn't feel that I was good enough to be there or that I had anything worthwhile to offer the Lord. My knees could only take about two and a half hours, and then I went to rejoin my district, still unresolved as to what I should do. Later that afternoon, though, I was summoned to the Branch President's office. This was it, I thought. The Lord must have told the Branch President that I should be sent home. I walked into his office expecting to hear, "Thanks, but no thanks." Instead, to my complete amazement, the Branch President called me to be his second counselor.

The Lord really was aware of my situation and knew what was best for me. Of all the wonderful experiences of my mission, the MTC has always stood out as perhaps the most growth-promoting of all. I learned and grew so much in the Gospel. My testimony increased by leaps and bounds, and my heart was filled to overflowing with humility and love.

I am so grateful for my mission and particularly for the MTC. I'm thankful that God doesn't mind using even the weakest of us in His work. I know that He gives no commandments to His children without preparing a way for them to accomplish them.

• • •

Whether you are headed for Lima, Peru; Lisbon, Portugal; or Detroit, Michigan your first stop (if you live in the United States and Canada) will be Provo, Utah, home of the Missionary Training Center (MTC). The Missionary Training Center is just what its name implies: a center for training missionaries — a boot camp of sorts. There you will be introduced to your mission. Of course, you won't be doing any real tracting, but you will have plenty of contact with the other very real elements of your mission. These include:

Prepare to Serve

- A companion who will be with you twenty-four hours a day. You will eat together, study together, pray together and collapse together in gym class.

- The proselyting discussions which you will begin studying your first or second day there. If you are learning them in your native tongue you will have memorized half of them by the end of your second week there. If you are learning them in Finnish or Navajo, you will have at least learned to say "Hello."

- A strict daily schedule which allows time for three square meals, personal and companion study, aerobic exercise, prayer and meditation, twelve hours of proselyting (or in this case, studying) and seven to eight hours of sleep.

- And (possibly) a foreign language which you will be required to speak reasonably well before you leave the MTC. When you start to dream in a foreign language, you know you are starting to understand it.

To show at a future family home evening, you might obtain from your local ward or branch the filmstrip *The Missionary Training Center: A Place for Preparation.* (15 minutes.) This slide show is shown to new missionaries the day they arrive at the MTC. If it is not available, you might ask a recently returned missionary to come talk at your family home evening about his or her Missionary Training Center experience.

With the exception of not doing any real proselyting, the missionary training center is an excellent place to introduce you to some of the realities of mission life. Right from the beginning you will be introduced to a companion who will be with you all the time. While a few missionaries will complain about having a constant companion, most learn that no one (themselves excepted) will have a greater effect on their success and happiness than their companion. The MTC will introduce you to the principle of learning to work closely with someone else and give you a preview of other things you will need to adjust to. You will also become acquainted with the missionary work and study schedule and daily exercise routine. If you are called to a foreign language mission, you will experience the utter frustration and inexpressible ecstasy that come with learning to communicate in another language.

Some of the returned missionaries at nearby BYU refer to the MTC as "spirit prison." But really the MTC acts as a vital buffer zone between you and full-fledged mission life. It helps you adjust to all of the previously mentioned elements in an environment that is more supportive and less bewildering. There, dedicated leaders and teachers will help you learn the language, adjust to your companion and mission schedule, and help you anticipate some differences in culture. They will especially help you develop effective teaching and proselyting skills. You will learn very early on that enjoying your missionary experience in the MTC depends very much on the same thing that enjoying the rest of your mission will — attitude.

If you live in an area that doesn't have access to the Provo MTC, you might attend a special MTC for your area or report directly to your mission. Don't think that missing out on the MTC will ruin your mission or make you any less of a missionary. There is nothing taught or learned at the MTC that you cannot learn on your own if you seek the Lord's help and are diligent. Having gone through the MTC experience myself, I'd say that 90 percent of what I learned was maturity. I felt like I was a horse being saddled and broke for the first time. It was not easy. But I am glad for the experience. By reading this book, and pursuing your own gospel study you will be light years ahead of another missionary who has just gone through the motions at the MTC. If you are worried about your capacity to teach, consider that most of the greatest missionaries of our dispensation didn't go to the MTC. Read Parley P. Pratt's autobiography and I think you will get the spirit of missionary work. It's not easy, it's demanding, it's tough, but it will be one of the most joyous and beautiful experiences of your life. You will be blessed with many enriching experiences because of your sacrifice to serve the Lord.

Prepare to Serve

So, whether you go to the MTC or prepare for your mission in another way, remember that your attitude and your diligence in preparing will determine the effectiveness and enjoyment of your missionary years.

Challenge

Obtain and read a copy of the pamphlet "The Missionary Training Center".

Diligently seek to prepare yourself for you mission by beginning to live missionary rules now.